T0130011

Mother Maria

Book I

God's Miracles
in
Lives of Regular People

TRILOGY

BOOK 1

Mother Maria

By Angelic Tarasio

GOD'S MIRACLES IN LIVES OF REGULAR PEOPLE

MOTHER MARIA

Author Credit: Tamara Kurbatov

Graphic Design Credits: Johny Ivanov

Photo detail: Painting in the background of the author is the work of art of His Highness Duke Michael David Peschka.

iUniverse books may be ordered through booksellers or by contacting:

iUniverse
1663 Liberty Drive
Bloomington, IN 47403
www.iuniverse.com
1-800-Authors (1-800-288-4677)

ISBN: 978-1-5320-8683-0 (soft cover)
ISBN: 978-1-5320-8684-7 (e-books)

Print information available on the last page.

iUniverse rev. date: 12/28/2019

I dedicate this book to my amazing
mother-in-law Maria,
Who was saved by the Divinity and who did
not separate her life from serving God,
The whole her life she kept rescuing
lost souls, like me,
Bringing us to God, our miraculous
Creator and Savior,
Our caring Father and merciful Protector,
Our only reliable Hope in this
hectic but wonderful world.
I wrote this book in honor of all of the people
Who suffered the hardships of World War II.

Author Angelic Tarasio

Foreword

I am writing this forward because I am German, I worked in Russia for many years, and I completed my postgraduate studies in the United States. My personal experience allows me to comprehend the significance of this book for modern day people of different countries and continents who are trying to succeed despite the hardships of life and search for fulfillment.

European people of my generation still have glimpses through family members into the experiences of people living during World War II. Some of us – depending on which side of the Iron Curtain we were born – have had personal experiences with the socialist regimes established in many countries of Europe after World War II. Great books are out there that not only describe but also make readers feel what life was like under totalitarian regimes in the 20th century. Nonetheless, there are certain aspects that make the trilogy *God's Miracles in Lives of Regular People* unique and a true revelation to its readers.

God's Miracles is **human**. Destinies of people on different sides of the political front are intertwined. In life threatening situations and great suffering, humanity and love stayed alive because in each system there were people who chose to be compassionate and above prejudice.

God's Miracles is **realistic**. It describes a fascinating life-story of a young woman from a noble family that resided in Western Ukraine. She survived and triumphed, being caught between two political regimes. Her family and she endured the destiny of being well-established and educated people who lost almost everything. Courage and true faith were the inner resources that helped the main character Maria overcome the hardships of the Nazi and Soviet camps, as well as the challenging life thereafter in the former Soviet Union.

God's Miracles is **spiritual**. The history of the family is a story of survival, full of wonders created by God and reinforced by true faith of mother Maria. The Divinity's support kept her alive. *God's Miracles* is not a book about suffering. It is a book about overcoming hardships and is an inspirational guidebook into life.

Michaela Schaefer, PhD
Top Management Consultant and
Executive Vice-President of German Top 100 Company

Preface

Can We Survive & Be Happy Under
the Pressure of Modern Life?

For 56 years of my life I was blessed with dying and surviving, with misfortune and happiness, and with incredibly interesting work, as a teacher, counselor, and holistic medicine practitioner I was also blessed with incredible life experiences that gave me the possibility to consider myself an expert in extremely difficult, life-threatening situations.

I wrote down the last sentence and smiled. Maybe, it would be easier for me not to undergo at least 50% of the hardships. Then who could call me an expert? An expert must know his subject, like nobody else. I wish that nobody else would learn my subject at such a high level of expertise.

I believe that every human being starts observing, encountering, or undergoing something from the very first moment of life. Many people consider that the gaining of life experience starts nine months prior to our appearance in the physical world. In my book, I do not discuss the equitableness of these theories. My major objective is to share with people the extraordinary life experience of my family in surviving hardships.

The development of mankind underwent different cycles. Everyone is familiar with the progressive augmentation in all the spheres of our society. The history of human life on the Earth contains intriguing historical facts. They influenced people in different times and ways: *positively*, when the spiritual, cultural, scientific, agricultural, and industrial development took place, or *negatively*, with the life-threatening events that brought the human society to the creation of non-democratic regimes, destructive wars with huge number of deaths, annihilation, and humiliation.

Mankind was blessed to survive the stressful and tragic events. Nothing new takes place nowadays. Society is on its next step of development, but the same human law, *"Survival of the Fittest"* works at all times.

So, you may think: how do you achieve the level of the fittest? Is it possible for everyone nowadays? Do we really need to develop our muscles in order to become fit? What makes people become fit? Why can one person succeed, and another cannot?

How was it possible, that a paralyzed child, our daughter, could survive five complicated surgeries, start regular school studies in the seventh grade, and achieve her first press-release, and all the possible school awards at the graduation from middle school? Due to her outstanding results, the attention of President Clinton was brought to the need of changing the law of academic American Legions' Award. Being in the eleventh grade, she became a college student. She was accepted as an extraordinarily talented child. Her majors were Metaphysics and Psychology.

Why are some of the healthy children completely lost from the first years of their school life? Why do twelve years of upsetting and stressful wandering in a forest of unlearned material not lead kids to the light, joy, knowledge, happiness, and the first important success in their life? Who teaches them happiness and compassion in life? Who teaches them always be connected with the Divinity? Who teaches them to rely only on the Divine forces and inner resources in difficult situations of their inexperienced life? They are taught a lot, but they are left internally undeveloped and unprotected. That is why they cannot survive the first hardships of life.

Fun is not life, and life is not fun. Children must learn this law at school in order to become the fittest and survive in the modern life. I taught our daughter to write nicely and to pay zero attention that her hands did not want to listen to her and were not able to hold a pen. We attached the pen to her hand, and she worked. Now, she writes her psycho-therapy notes for hours and is always grateful to God who blessed her with patience and challenging work.

The scary facts about suicide alarm modern society. It became the third leading cause of death among 15- to 24-year olds. Suicide-related behaviors among U.S. high school students, grades 9-12, in 2007 reached 14.5% of students. They seriously considered suicide for 12 months of their life.

Global changes in finance and economics, political instability and years of uncertainty, unfortunate relationships and inability to find support and happiness in life, make people depressed. It is not a secret that every one of the people who committed suicide was depressed. I can understand that life is not always a piece of cake, but I do not believe that we should give up at the very first sign of suffering. If it were so, then I should have been deeply depressed for at least thirty years of my life.

We celebrated our daughter's 1st birthday, and in a short while, my father passed away at the age of 57 from lung cancer. He was a wonderful father, and I miss him for the rest of my life. In two months following my father's death, my husband got into a car crash. Conventional medicine did not find it possible to help him with multiple skeletal fractures, including the spine, and injuries of the internal organs. Nevertheless, he was blessed to survive.

What prevented him from deep depression and suicide, when he was paralyzed for a year? What gave him strength to start walking again, falling 25-30 times a day, and being for half a year constantly bruised? What forced him to go to the Chinese monastery and stay there for nearly four years? He promised the Lord, if he survived, then he would serve God, saving the lives of God's children.

He realized that nobody, other than God, helped his mother to find and bring the Chinese healer. A miracle happened, and after he was able to move slowly without my help, he left to learn the art of Eastern Medicine healing and stayed there until he mastered it. Later, he became a well-known practitioner, with established practice in Philadelphia. His clients arrived to see him and undergo his treatment from different states of the USA, Canada, and Europe.

What pushed countless people to commit suicide? There was a wonderful article by Patricia Cohen in The New York Times, where a thoughtful author tried to attract the attention of readers to the problem of suicide in our society. The answer for the question as to why it became a frequent practice in our highly developed society was undefined. The programs of the American Association of Suicidology cannot prevent the suicide and suicide attempts, and more than 395,000 people with serious self-inflicted injuries are treated in emergency rooms every year. Suicide also affects the life of the society, planting and growing fear, shock, guilt, and the same depression among family members and friends.

The number that found federal Center for Disease Control and Prevention is unmerciful: the suicide rate among 45-to-54-year-olds increased nearly 20% from 1999 to 2004. That was the time before financial chaos of 2008. Why did we lose our physically healthy children, parents, relatives, and friends? My question was not answered by years of studying the problem, as a teacher and holistic medicine practitioner.

Now there is a period of severe instability in human life. I was reading the material on Bankruptcy Filing.

The Bankruptcy statistics go with the annual rate of 1.3 million filings in 2008. Huge numbers of people have lost their businesses, employment, steady income, established position in society, as well as understanding and respect of their families.

What will work for these people? Will they be susceptible to depression under the growing pressures of modern life? That was one of the reasons, why I wrote my books at the present time. I wanted to show people that real life danger, misfortune, suppression, and poverty existed in different countries and at different times. The people underwent them with God's blessing. The main purpose of my work is enlightening people and supporting them during the time of hardship, so that they can discover the fullness of life.

God's miracles happen every day. They have happened to everyone in my family. They will happen to you. Ask and you will receive. The Lord will support you to become the fittest in this life.

Author Angelic Tarasio
Florida, USA

Introduction

I consider myself a happy person. My life wasn't easy. However, all the challenges from youth to the present moment did not break me physically, spiritually and psychologically. God blessed me to pass one life test after another, and every time, my relatives and friends asked the same question: How could I manage?

They saw that all my hardships were awarded with miraculous results. Sometimes, it has already happened, but it was difficult for the regular observers to believe that it was successfully resolved, and I was able to go through it. My dear readers, I am close to sharing my secret with you.

I think that the first God's real miracle occurred to me when I met my husband Tikhon, and his mother Maria. On the first day in their family, I identified that my mother-in-law belonged to another world. There was no earthly force that could extinguish her faith and love for God.

She did not judge me for being atheist. I came from the military family, where the word "God" was prohibited, as it was prohibited in the whole communist society. With time, my mother-in-law became my first teacher in theology, my older sister in Faith, and my dear friend in life. She did not pretend that she served God - she was not able to separate her life from serving the Divinity. Thank You, Lord, for sending mother-in-law Maria into my life. She brought me to God, as His child, and it was she who opened the door for me to human spirituality and hope.

Years passed. We enjoyed mother Maria's visits. Our children were thrilled to listen to her stunning reading of the tales. Nobody could read the tales, as dramatic, as she did. The kids were in beds at 8 in the evening, when the theater of one actor started her performance.

Before 8 p.m., it was my time with mother Maria. We prayed together, cooked our favorite dishes, knitted or crochet. One day, mother Maria mentioned to me that she was writing the journals during many years of her life. On that very day, she added a personal information that was shocking for me. My mother-in-law stated, "I began to write my dairies after the discharge from the force labor camp GULAG. I don't know, why I took a risk to do it. My children did not want me to write. They said, whatever had happened to me was my past. On that time, millions of soviet people went through it. Maybe, they are right."

I sensed that mother Maria did not agree with the opinion of her children and asked to read her journals. The information that I learned from her diaries, turned up-side-down the whole world for me. Everyone who had university education studied a subject "History of the communism". Nobody gave us the truth that I found in my mother-in-law's journals.

She secretly wrote a diary for many years of her thorny life. She cut the regular 24-page school notebooks in half along the page, putting on the cover the next number of a journal. I asked her, why she could not use a notebook without cutting. Mother Maria explained: "I wrote the notes in a format that could easily be hidden under the armrests of the sofa." I was on summer vacation when mother Maria gave me the opportunity to read her notebooks, two at a time.

Mother Maria assumed that I was ready to read her diaries in my early thirties. To my opinion, she was not sure that being any younger, I was able to comprehend the depth of her enlightenment and understand the facts and events she described there. When she saw, how fast I read every part of her journal, mother Maria brought the idea of writing a book about the life of her family. She knew that there was no way to publish the book in the communist country. When God gave us the possibility to leave the USSR, she brought the journals again, and we read them together with her personal explanation of the data.

I understood the records better after her personal interpretation. The communist authorities would never like her writing, although she learned to record the events without emotional or self-pitying description. She mentioned the facts in a chain of timing, recording everything in days, weeks, months, and years.

Her life was not a regular human life. The events, she went through were so dramatic, and yet at the same time, they were everyday occurrences in soviet society in the 30s, 40s, and 50s during the 20th century. I "swallowed" the journals fast for one to two days, and then brought them back to her. In return, she gave me another two notebooks, asking every time to be careful with them.

I understood why mother Maria was so nervous about my reading her chronicles. Many family facts described in the diaries were new to me, and she was not sure whether I could understand them correctly. The last thing she wanted was that my reading of her diaries could negatively affect our relationship with Tikhon. On the contrary, it helped me understand my husband better after learning the history of his family.

Mother Maria was pleased watching, how I was astonished with everything she recorded. One day, she mentioned that she would like us, her children, to write a book, describing in details all the events of their lives. She provided me with the main concept: "I want the book to be written in such a way that people believe that God's miracles happen in the lives of regular people. Otherwise, how can you explain the fact that we have met and are all together? Only Divine forces did not allow the evil to destroy our family."

Being her daughter in-law, I did not realize that she wanted me to fulfill the task of writing and publishing a book. It took 23 years before I sensed a persistent desire to write a book about God's miracles with which three generations of our family were blessed. My mother-in-law's dream came true. Being a linguist, but not a professional writer, I did my best. My book is a work of not a complete fiction. I used the dated chain of events from mother-in-law Maria's diary and described them using her interpretation of the facts and my imagination. The true story of my mother-in-law became the keystone of the trilogy. The chain of miraculous events happened, as described. However, most of the names, places, characters, I used fictitiously, and any resemblance to actual living or dead person or places of the events are entirely coincidental.

Author Angelic Tarasio,

Chapter 1

My mother-in-law, Countess Maria Kotyk-Kurbatov, was born in 1919 into a relatively wealthy and well-educated Ukrainian family. The family estate, Blakytni Strumky (Blue Creeks), was located in western Ukraine that belonged to Poland at the time and had not yet fallen under the control of the soviet regime. Her father Count, Lukian Kotyk, was a physician who had graduated from the leading medical schools in Poland and England.

After Lukian's successful graduation, his father, Count Leon Kotyk, purchased him, as graduation gifts, an estate in Blue Creeks, a picturesque area near Lvov, a light carriage, and four strong and beautiful horses – a pair for the carriage and a pair for riding. The old Count Kotyk trusted his son and was sure that a gentleman of twenty-eight was ready for an interesting life. The close location to Lvov made the life of Dr. Kotyk, Jr. very impressive. Every week he visited theater performances, exhibitions, concerts, or lectures in medicine and science.

The old Count wanted his son to build his own medical practice. He himself had been already in that field for thirty-four years. It was not easy to stand at the operating table or to visit and treat patients with complicated medical conditions day in and day out for so many years. He was happy to have reliable support in the area and was pleased watching how knowledgeable and serious his son was in his work. The father was proud of him, listening to the stories of his neighbors regarding different successful cases of a young doctor. His son was ready to help his patients at any time. People could meet his light carriage everywhere in the area. There were a couple of cases when the weather was nasty and the roads were treacherous due to weekly rains, but the young doctor managed to see his patients, riding his new horse. Devotion to the professional field was the major family inheritance.

Maria's mother, Countess Anna Dobrensky-Kotyk, belonged to another noble Ukrainian family from the beautiful area of the Carpathian Mountains. She had a very attractive appearance, with the facial features of a Carpathian beauty. She was slender, with a slightly swarthy complexion, dark black eyebrows, long eyelashes, and glaring hazel eyes. Her hair could be her pride; she had two long thick braids down to the knees.

Anna was an orphan when Dr. Lukian Kotyk met her. Anna's mother passed away on the second day after Anna was born. Her father died when the girl was fourteen. Anna had three older brothers. After her father's death, she moved to the house of her oldest brother Orest, and lived with his family in a magnificent castle on Blue Creek, ten miles west from the estate of Count Kotyk, Jr.

Count Lukian Kotyk met Anna when she was seventeen. Her brother had invited him for winter hunting.

The young doctor was impressed with the beauty of the neighbor's sister. With time, Lukian Kotyk became the most frequent visitor of the Dobrensky family, and after the church service on Sundays, he used to be invited for lunch. Dr. Kotyk liked his visits to the Dobrensky family and cherished the time spent in the friendly atmosphere of his neighbors. He also enjoyed the long walks and conversations with the beautiful and smart Ms. Anna. She spent her days reading books, playing the piano, and singing. She had an impressive voice and everyone liked her singing very much. The young beauty did not refuse to sing for Count Kotyk, watching with a lady's pleasure how he admired her and her songs.

Anna sensed that the young Count felt her loneliness and was sorry for her. He had also lost his mother when he was five years of age and always missed her very much. Like all young ladies, she dreamed to meet somebody who could make her life brighter. Anna's heart raced when she saw him standing in the church next to her brother. Anna noticed that she awaited his visits after church. It was a real joy for the young lady when she saw his carriage on a weekday after he had finished visiting the patients in their area. Anna complained,

"Why do you so seldom visit the patients from our area? Are all of them healthy?"

Count Kotyk looked at Anna with understanding and explained,

"Another doctor has practice in your area, and I am here only when he invites me for consultations to have second opinion."

In 1918, two weeks after the Easter holiday, the priest of the local church made an announcement: "Count Lukian Kotyk proposed marriage to the Countess Anna Dobrensky."

The wedding was planned to be at the end of August, and the couple decided to spend their honeymoon in Italy and France. Everything was arranged in the best way, and the young couple came back not in a month, but by the end of winter. Anna was pregnant with her first daughter Maria. Nobody had ever seen Anna laughing so much. She was singing and playing the piano for hours, and her songs were heard all over the Kotyk's mansion. They loved each other and God blessed them with four children spanning over the next ten years.

In seven months, after the giving birth to their fourth child, little Jennie, something happened to Anna. She did not look happy and became unusually *quiet*. Since then, no one heard her laugh or sing. Dr. Kotyk, being a physician, rationalized to himself that four pregnancies over ten years exhausted his wife, and she needed a nice rest in a warm and sunny climate.

Anna left for Capri to spend three winter months there. Dr. Kotyk could not accompany his wife because of the severe epidemic of strep throat in the area with hundreds of fatal cases, as well as his two younger children who were unusually frequently sick during that winter after the strep throat infection.

In the spring of 1929, Anna arrived home by herself. She looked very well and seemed as if she were glad to be at home again and see her children, although there was something amiss in her attitude towards her husband. She avoided talking and being with him. No longer did they take long walks in the evening, or engage in long conversations in their sitting room. Anna refused to sleep in their bedroom, explaining that she missed Jennie so much that she preferred to sleep in the narrow nanny's bed in Jennie's room. She refused to visit Lvov theaters or see their friends.

Dr. Kotyk suffered, watching the shifts in the behavior of his wife. He kept hoping that with time, his love and patience could melt the ice in their relationship, and Annie would be his wife again. Everyone in the house prepared for the Ester holidays. Anna refused to visit her elder brother Orest for Easter, so Dr. Kotyk invited all her brothers and their families to Creeks.

He wanted to make a pleasant surprise for his wife to cheer her up. One day before the Easter holiday, the family gathered together. The old Count Kotyk arrived in the morning and brought many gifts to his grandchildren. He helped Lukian meet the rest of the guests. The old Count noticed the tension in the house and asked,

"Is everything all right with you?"

When nobody answered him, he sensed that something was definitely wrong.

The tension was slightly relieved by the children, who were sincerely happy to see their cousins. The children played on the floor with a new railway train set, brought by Grandpa, never suspecting that it was their last holiday together.

After lunch on the second day of the holiday, Anna's brothers decided to explain everything to Lukian Kotyk. They considered it unfair to keep in secret the true reason for all the changes in his wife. Lukian invited the brothers-in-law to his study room. When the four of them took their seats, the younger brother, Michael, reminded,

"Do you remember, Lukian, Anna's visit to our place on St. Irena's day? It was Irena's birthday. She turned three.

Lukian remembered that day very well. Anna was Irena's Godmother, and they planned to go there together. The carriage waited at the entrance of the house. At that time, a man was delivered with an extremely dangerous trauma in his leg that required surgery. Dr. Kotyk had to stay, and Anna left with the children. Lukian listened attentively to Michael's story.

"At the party, Anna met my friend Oleg from Canada. She remembered Oleg from her childhood. We were neighbors and as kids, we spent a lot of time playing together. When Anna was thirteen, Oleg's parents moved to Canada. Since then, she had not heard anything about him. Our sister and Oleg were excited recalling their childhood. By the end of the evening, Anna and Oleg realized that they remembered everything very well and missed each other for all the fifteen years since they had last seen one another."

It was hard for Lukian to listen to the prelude of his misfortune. His thoughts were climbing in chaos. All of them brought him to the same conclusion, "Why should I listen to them? I need to talk to Anna. We can clarify everything. We can always understand each other."

Michael perceived Lukian's impatience. He added, "Everyone noticed that the memory of childhood engaged both of them, but nobody was ready to hear a statement at the end of the party that they suffered all fifteen years because life separated them."

Lukian watched Michael for a while and then asked, "Is he married?"

"Oleg mentioned that he was married, but was not happy and felt lonely in the coldness of Canada. Anna started feeling sorry for him at first, but eventually those feelings turned into something stronger. Everything had changed so quickly. She was in a whirlpool of his life and did not want to escape. By the end of the visit, Anna and Oleg could not imagine their lives without each other."

Lukian looked at the men in the room and asked a question that Anna's brothers were ready to hear,

"Gentlemen, what do you think of me? No, we should not even talk about me! What is going to happen with our children? What should I explain to them? Should I mention them that their mother forgot about eleven years of happiness, motherhood, and commitment for one evening spent with a visitor from Canada? What if you, gentlemen, are mistaken about everything?"

The eldest brother Orest was nervous most of all. Anna grew up in his house and she got married to an honest and honorable man. Orest was happy for his sister. What happened in the end? She destroyed her life, as well as the lives of her husband and children. He felt sorry for Lukian. Orest considered Lukian his best friend. However, they should not hide the truth. Orest brought the unmerciful verdict:

"We feel sorry for you, Lukian, your children, and the whole situation. Anna is under a spell. She does not hear us. She constantly repeats, 'I am in love. I cannot live without him.' We tried to intervene, but were unsuccessful. She does not look well and we are afraid that we can lose her. Nobody wants a tragedy to take place. We decided to move to Canada, and Anna expressed her desire to go with us. Forgive her, Lukian if you can, but let her go."

Lukian ran out of the room. He could not believe the words of Anna's brothers. He wanted to talk to his Annie. He wanted her to explain everything to him. Count Kotyk found Anna in the playroom. He came up to his wife when she was playing with younger children and asked,

"Children, I am sorry to interrupt, but I am taking your Mama for a while. Play with your cousins and madam Cherry."

The four children looked at their parents, feeling with their souls the unbearable pain of the big father's soul that was ready to rupture. Lukian took Anna to their sitting room that was near their bedroom and asked his wife to take a seat. He did not want to start the unpleasant conversation. He loved her so much. He did not have enough air to breathe since the "verdict" was announced.

For a minute or two, Lukian was admiring Anna's pale face, slim build, and gentle complexion. More than anything else, he wanted to hide his face in her hair again, to breathe the miraculous smell of wild flowers. Each time, the smell of her hair made him excited and he sank in love and loved her with all his passion that nature blessed him with.

Presently, they sat together, as they used to do every day for eleven years of their married life. He wanted to look into her eyes and move closer.

"Annie, the situation we are in is not easy. I do not want you to leave. I would like you to stay for a while in order to learn more of what is going on. I can understand that you lost interest in me and fell in love with another man. Perhaps I had some fault in it: I was too busy and did not spend enough time with you. What do you think about our four children, Annie? The children are very young and they need their mother."

Anna was sitting with her head down, looking at her hands. She did not want to raise her head and look at him. His voice trembled.

"Annie, I am not talking about you and me. Be merciful to the children. What can we say to them? What should I answer when they ask me about you? Can you wait for a year, at least? We will prepare the children for the tragic changes in their lives. It is difficult for me to handle such a shock, and what about our children!"

Anna looked at her husband, with eyes full of fear,

"A year? Do you mean that I have to be here for another year? I cannot wait for another day or even an hour, and you want me to wait for a year? I shall die in a month, if I stay. You want me to die, don't you?"

She became angry with him. Her voice trembled with fury, condemnation, rage, and even hatred. He looked into her eyes. They were not the eyes of his beloved Annie. They were not hazel anymore, but had turned black.

Lukian understood that there was no place for him and his children in the heart of such a cold woman. There was no power on earth to keep her in the family. The thoughts climbed, one on the top of the other.

"Annie, mon amour, how could your children become unimportant to you? My love doesn't mean anything for you either."

He looked at the face of his wife. She was offended with his suggestion. It was the face of a stranger. He did not want that stranger to be here. The stranger would never be his Annie again. They could not be happy together. His thoughts circled around the children. Then he found the inner strength and pulled himself together, making a conclusion,

"If she is not happy with us, it is better to let her go. If she decides to return in some time, I will try not to shut out my heart. I love Anna and that's my misfortune."

Count Kotyk put his hands on her shoulders and pronounced in a clear voice,

"Anna, you forgot about God. As a wife, you dishonored me. As a mother, you betrayed your children. Now I do not want you to stay here. You are free to go. You can pack and leave today."

His heart was racing, "My Anna left him for another man. What could be worse?"

The Count opened the door of their sitting room and turned around.

"Thank you for eleven years of my life - eleven years of happiness and joy. You became a traitor, Anna, but I wish you good luck."

In the spring of 1930, Anna immigrated to Canada with her brothers. The children were raised by their father. The nannies and a French governess were good assistance for Count Kotyk. All of the kids missed their mother in accordance with the time they spent with her. The youngest, Jennie and Leon stopped talking and asking about her approximately a month after she left. The other two children, Maria and Vassily, waited for her for years and in their morning prayers, they asked God to return their mother, as soon as possible.

Glory to Thee, o Lord! Glory to Thee!

Chapter 2

In September of 1930, Count Kotyk took Maria to Lvov convent school to continue her studies there. The girl found good teachers and sincere nuns at school, and they helped Maria forgive her mother and release some pain out of the child's soul. Maria was a talented student who was interested in everything: languages, history, math, and science. She was one of the best in music and singing. She was absolutely the best in handcraft: knitting, sewing, and embroidering. Her father and grandfather were proud of her. By age sixteen, she became an exact copy of her mother, a real beauty, and a talented young lady.

By 1936, Countess Maria Kotyk had graduated from the convent school. Her childhood dream was to follow her father and grandfather into the medical profession, and she was offered a place at the Sorbonne University to study medicine. Maria decided to spend one summer month at her grandfather's estate with her best friend, Anastasia, before starting her University studies. Anastasia had also won a place at the Sorbonne medical school. In early June, the pair arrived at the old Count Kotyk estate full of anticipation and excitement at the prospect of starting their adult lives in two months. Both girls planned to leave for France by the end of August.

Maria's grandfather, Count Leon Kotyk, was in his eighties and lived by himself in his own charming mansion, twelve miles from his son. Dr. Leon was a very tall, strong and still handsome man, with thick gray hair and a bushy mustache. He enjoyed wearing linen shirts with beautiful embroidery on the collar.

The old count liked to spend most of the warm, summer days outside. When he stayed in his mansion, he would sit in a huge old leather armchair on the porch of his beautiful house, praying and listening to the beautiful birdsongs and other sounds of nature. The birds in the Ukraine chirped their songs like talented and well-practiced singers who were ready to sing their parts in a chorus or a famous fairy-tale performance. However, most of all he enjoyed wandering the entire day in the forest, gathering herbs for his remedies.

Maria was accustomed to meeting people on her grandfather's estate. They came from miles around to receive his medical consultations and herbal remedies. Some visitors asked the old count to read for them a passage from the Old or New Testament, for reading of which he had a special talent. As a child, Maria liked listening to these readings, but most of all she enjoyed the way, how her grandfather was able to interpret the readings and connect them with the daily lives of the listeners. It was a special kind of preaching, and only her grandpa knew how to do it.

One morning after breakfast during that summer, Maria's friend Anastasia asked the old count to read to her. He did so with pleasure. Then, he prophesized her bright future that he saw clearly while reading the passage from the Holy Bible. Anastasia was destined for success in her studies, a happy marriage, and the continuation of her Austrian heritage. Anastasia was very excited and kissed the old count. Everything was supposed to come true. She knew that she was ready for studies in one of the best schools. She was engaged at sixteen and ready for marriage in a year and a half. She learned about her heritage in Austria two months ago.

Maria wanted to learn what she was blessed and destined for. Standing behind her grandfather's armchair with her arms around his neck, she listened with eyes opened wide to her grandfather's interpretation of the passage he had read for her from the Holy Gospel. Each word etched itself deeply into her heart,

"You will be on fire, yet not burned down. You will be drowning in water, yet not be drowned. You will be kept in bitter cold, but never be frozen. The crowd will trample and torment your body, but you shall survive. You will be a mother of three children without a husband and scarcely know the taste of a woman's happiness. The only good thing I see for you, darling, is that our Savior and his Virgin Mother will support you, and later your enemies will admit and admire your dignity, knowledge, and talents."

Maria was shocked, and when her grandfather opened his eyes and turned around to behold his granddaughter, he looked deeply upset.

Hardly a day passed when the girls did not discuss the old count's readings. Maria refused to believe her grandfather's vision. Like all the young Mademoiselles, she dreamed of happiness and romance. If she had not been loved by her mother, who left her years ago, then she had to deserve to meet a handsome and brave prince. There were no signs of danger in the idyllic surrounding of her grandpa's estate: deep blue sky, thick birch, oak and pine forests, green meadows, and the fields with bright green silky grass and flowers. Beautiful white, red, blue, and yellow flowers as far as the eye could see.

Maria even felt reproachful.

"Why was my grandfather so optimistic about Anastasia and so pessimistic about me?"

The girl could not get rid of the thought. As the days went on, she thought more about what her grandfather had foreseen. She wanted summer to be over. Maria was eager to prove to the old Count that he was wrong and she convinced herself that nothing and no one could harm her once she started her new life in the famous school in Paris, far away from her grandfather's home.

Four years of studies in France flew past very quickly at full tilt. In the spring of 1940, Maria was nearly twenty-year-old beautiful young Mademoiselle, who had graduated, as a physician, from the Sorbonne Medical School. She prepared to marry Count Alexander Kurbatov, the prince of her dreams. They already had their Betrothal church ceremony. Maria knew that the Betrothal part of a church wedding was the most important in Christianity. From that moment forth, she belonged to Alexander, her dearest Alex, and he belonged to her. Everything seemed perfect for the young doctor Maria Kotyk – far, very far away from her grandfather's predictions. Her life was clear and wonderful, except the broadcast news. Trouble was brewing in the background.

The radio brought only disturbing and frightening information. Hitler's expansionist intentions were declared to the whole world. The soviet government was about to move to "unite" all of the Ukraine under the red banner of workers and peasants, and to "align" the borders in the Baltic countries. They started their war against Finland.

It was difficult for Maria to understand the significance of all the changes in her homeland and the Baltic countries. Even her father for the first time in Maria's life was not able to answer clearly her questions. He tried to appear calm at her engagement party, but at the same time, he strongly opposed Maria's coming home before the wedding, explaining vaguely because the peasants lost their meekness. Maria reluctantly agreed to obey his wishes, but with the slightest sense that the idyllic world of her beautiful Ukrainian life might be damaged or destroyed and never be the same.

The young Countess still needed to complete half a year of practical work in a hospital under the supervision of experienced doctors before she could start her own practice. Where would she have her residency? Although of Russian noble descent, her fiancé was born in France, and he intended to remain there, but Maria remembered the successful medical practice of her grandfather and father in the Ukraine and was enthusiastic to return "home" and help the local people in their hour of need. In her dreams, Maria saw herself working for her father, assisting in surgeries and providing the home visits.

Even in Paris, the situation had been tense during the last year. An air of anxious expectation hung over everyone. Some of the fellow-students from Poland and Czechoslovakia had dropped out of school in the middle of the school year and left with their parents and siblings for England, America, and other farther-flung destinations.

Almost every day Maria's mind was wandering through the forests and meadows that belonged to her family. Maria often pondered, "How could it be possible to feel insecure at our estate? We had never harmed anyone. We provided a quiet and decent life for the villagers. My father and grandfather had always been there to treat the sick people."

Maria did not allow the fearful thoughts and feelings to possess her mind. She wanted to believe that nothing could happen to her native land. Her classmates from Spain described how their beautiful country lay in ruins with over a million dead. Maria thought, "Now the civil war in Spain is over I am sure the politicians can find a way to thwart Hitler and Mussolini's aggressive intentions. Then we can live in peace again. We can love, work, dance, deliver children into this world, and feel happy every day."

The young lady did not know that Hitler was about to start his war against all the European countries and that his troops were ready to move fast, conquering new territories, bringing death and suffering to millions of people. Maria agreed to undergo the practical part of her studies in Paris, but insisted on going home to spend at least a month of summer in her Creeks.

She missed her home because she had not been there since the summer with Anastasia. Maria spent a month every summer with her father, brothers, and Jennie in Greece where the Kotyks resided in their summerhouse on the Mediterranean Sea. It was nice there, but the young Countess missed her Ukrainian home.

Even when she dreamed of home, the recollection of her last visit still tinged with resentment of her grandfather's reading. However, looking at her present life, Maria felt vindicated. Grandpa's interpretation has not turned out to be true.

"That was his misreading," Maria thought. She wanted to believe in it.

Maria purchased the train ticket for April 24, 1940. On the train from Paris to Lvov Maria caught herself repeating from time to time the same prayer, *"Help us, save us, have mercy on us and keep us, O Lord, by Thy grace."* She was surprised, "Why am I repeating this prayer constantly?"

She remembered that she had been vaguely conscious of a strange pain in her heart as she looked out of the window, waving goodbye to her fiancé at the platform of the station.

She clearly remembered Alexander standing there in his new white linen suit, white sandals, and white hat. He was a very handsome young man: tall with a well-developed athletic figure. His big blue eyes and dark eyelashes had attracted the attention of many young Mademoiselles who observed the happy couple with envy.

Maria knew that he was strongly against her trip to Ukraine. They had modified a new route due to the German occupation of Poland in September of 1939, and the trip was longer than usual, with additional changes of trains due to new itinerary. Alexander was afraid that if the war broke out further in Europe, they might lose each other for a long time, if not forever. She promised to be back by the end of July to start her apprenticeship in the hospital where Alex had already worked for two years as a general surgeon. Maria looked at her gorgeous engagement ring and felt a pang of guilt,

"Poor Alex, he was so upset with my decision to visit the Ukraine now."

Maria tried to find the excuses why she did not listen to her father, Alex, and her future mother in-law regarding the danger of the trip.

"I miss my little sister Jennie and younger brothers, my mansion, my room, and the view from my balcony. I like France, but it is different there. They do not have forests and meadows like ours. It is time for berries. I want to go to our forest again and to gather and smell fresh berries."

At that moment, it seemed to Maria that the smell of fresh, wild raspberries drifted through the carriage. Maria closed her eyes. She smiled and continued dreaming:

"I want to fall down in the thick emerald grass and feel the silky, juicy stems of the grass between my fingers. Every day I will bring home fresh field flowers and place them around our house. I want to wear my Ukrainian blouse that Jennie's nanny Ganja embroidered for me. Papa told me how Ganja had sewn and embroidered a new one for each of us for Easter, including him and grandpa. Ganja knew our favorite colors and using them she made the same pattern look different."

The young Countess sank deeper into recollection. She remembered the Ukrainian sky that she had always found absolutely magical. She could stare into it for hours. When she was eleven and they were sitting on the balcony, she described it to her father.

"Look, it is made of sapphire velvet at night, covered with thousands of small and large diamonds. Sometimes it looks like I can jump up and touch them."

Her father burst into laughter and asked what she could say about the sky during the day. Maria replied,

"Papa, I used to lie down on the grass behind the house looking at the blue sky for a long time. I tried to see our Lord and His Mother there: I wanted to ask them about our Mama. But I've seen only fluffy white clouds in the silky blue sky. I could read them, Papa! They had shapes of different animals, mountains, forests, and fantastic creatures from the fairylands."

Emerging from her reverie, Maria could not help acknowledging that her justifications were childish and capricious. Then she considered more serious things.

"I can help my Dad in his practice. He needs some help. It will be very beneficial for my professional experience and helpful for him."

She sighed, looking again at the sparkling diamond of her engagement ring. Once again, Maria thought of Alexander who wanted to accompany her, but his mother's health condition had not allowed it.

Alexander's father, Count Sergey Kurbatov passed away in February of 1940. Since then, Alexander's mother had fallen ill. Madam Kurbatova used to be very active and strong, but the death of her husband affected her greatly. Her heart condition seriously deteriorated. Last week she started to walk out of their chateau with the help of Millen, her helpful maid.

They were a wonderful couple. After the funeral, Madam Kurbatova stayed in bed for a month. Then she started to walk out from her bedroom to the balcony to sit there and pray for the soul of her beloved husband. She asked the Lord to forgive her husband all the sins and make a place for him in heaven. The Countess was sure that her husband was not severely sinful. She used to say,

"Marie, for the whole my life, he was like my Guardian angel, and he was an example of honor and generosity to our Alexander."

Maria used to think, "They lived decent and honorable life. I wish to have the same type of relationship with my husband. What can be more important? My father suffers all his life. He loved, but Maman did not love him. She did not love us as well. I grew up with pain in my heart for my father, brothers, Jennie, and myself. Thank God, I fell in love. I trust Alexander. I think he will be like his father in marriage.

It was a surprise to Maria, when in just a week after her arrival, her father and grandfather insisted on her returning to France! Maria was certain that their worries that she was in danger if she stayed at the family estate, were exaggerated. She tried to assert them that she definitely needed to stay longer in order to celebrate with the family her twentieth birthday on July 4, 1940.

One morning she was awoke with an animated conversation in French taking place under the balcony. The balcony door was slightly open, allowing the fresh spring breeze to float into Maria's bedroom. She recognized both voices. Her father was talking to the local priest who had brought the terrible news and asked her father for advice.

"Dr. Kotyk, what should we do? Where can we go away? How can we defend our families, land, faith, history, and our lives? The German troops occupied the territory of Poland and they brought their "ordnung" there – barbarian order and death. Now the soviets are absorbing our regions."

Maria turned to stone. She heard the reply of her father.

"There is no place where we can disappear, Father Bogdan. I realized that we got into the crossfire of two dangerous political systems: fascist and communist. Both of them are demonically totalitarian. They disagree with anything that differs from their inhuman laws."

The priest continued.

"Oh, yes, Dr. Kotyk, the NKVD thoroughly enforces their armed regime, including imprisoning and executing. Hundreds of citizens from Rivne, Ostrig, Sambir, Stryi, Drogobych, and Ternopil had been arrested and sent to Siberian camps. The lands, banks, factories, plants, stores, hotels, and houses were expropriated. They secretly destroyed seven big cathedrals, and five priests were shot."

Dr. Kotyk said,

"The whole world became more evil than ever. I heard what Nazis did to Jews in Poland. They decided to annihilate the nation and the world cannot stop them."

Maria had immediately remembered Sofia. Maria's father had a housekeeper Sofia Kogan, a Jewish woman, who helped Dr. Kotyk with the household after the departure of Anna Dobrensky. She was a kind woman, who loved the children better than their mother. The children loved Sofia dearly. Sofia was a widow. Her husband died when her daughter Rosa was five years old. Since then she worked for Count Kotyk's family.

Sofia was a devoted person and ran the household with great efficiency, ensuring that the other staff's work was up to scratch. Some of the servants were a little bit afraid of her supervision, because she could see all the defects in their work. The servants could find some relief on Saturdays. Everyone in the family accepted the fact that Sofia and her daughter Rosa did not work on Saturdays. It was the day, when they used to go to the synagogue and visit their family in the nearest town. It was established as a rule at Count Kotyk's estate, and a mother and daughter knew that they were part of a big family.

Maria felt sorry about herself and her arrival. She wanted to leave, to be further from the confusion and danger. She did not want to stay any longer at her estate.

"The next day the soviets come and the estate would be expropriated, as many others," Maria thought.

Maria started to pack, thinking,

"Back to France, back to my Alexander. O Lord, why did I come? I would like to be far away from all the barbarian changes."

Dr. Kotyk knocked on the door of Maria's bedroom.

"Come in, Papa."

He was surprised to see his daughter packing.

"I decided to follow your advice, Papa and to leave for France. After breakfast I would like us to go to the Lvov railway station, and we'll buy a ticket for the first train that goes to Paris."

Dr. Kotyk looked at Maria attentively and noticed that the balcony door was open.

"You have heard our conversation with father Bogdan, haven't you?"

Maria came up to her father, put her arms around his neck, and put her head on his chest. The father stroked her hair, as he used to do when she was a small girl.

"I am afraid, Papa. I cannot understand anything, but I am afraid. Let us all pack and leave. You can stay in Greece or you can buy a house in France. Papa, let us all go together. It is too dangerous to keep the family in

Creeks. They can come here tomorrow or the day after tomorrow. Where will you go?"

Dr. Kotyk answered,

"Marie, I thought about it many times. If the worst comes to worst and the soviets come to take away our estate, I would take the children to grandfather's hunting lodge in the woods."

"Dad, why don't you want to leave the country? They need to attend school, to live a free life, and to be not hidden anywhere in the forests. If they find you, what will happen then?"

Dr. Kotyk smiled.

"Marie, we have changed our roles, right? Don't worry, my girl. If I see real danger for the children, I will leave for Greece and let you know about it. But who could be sure that any country in Europe is a secure place to stay?"

They did not talk much at breakfast. Then her father announced about Maria's departure and the siblings accompanied Maria to the carriage. She looked at them and tears poured down her cheeks. Vassily was a strong and handsome young man. He easily helped Maria with her luggage. Maria saw her father coming to take her to the train. She kissed her brothers and Jennie and took her seat in the carriage. They had gone already far from Creeks, but Maria could not stop crying, praying repetitively, *"Lord, have mercy!"*

The railway station in Lvov looked unusually crowded on that day. There were long lines to buy tickets, but all the booking offices were closed. People tried to leave the country. Fear and uncertainty drove people from their homes. They left everything. Taking only their children, they tried to escape from the dangerous zone as quickly as possible. The announcements were repetitive; all the trains were cancelled due to the military operations of the soviet army that was on its mission for liberation of the former Ukrainian territories of Bessarabia, Bukovina, Galicia, and Volhynia, taken in 1918 by Rumania and Poland. Dr. Kotyk met his old friend and found out that due to military operations and war in Europe, there was no more train connection with Paris. It was cancelled two days ago. Maria felt trapped.

Their journey back home was unusually long and scary. Maria could not change anything, and her future, as well as the future of her whole family, was unpredictable. When the house was seen from a distance, Dr. Kotyk said,

"Marie, I did not want you to come. I wanted you to live in France and be happy there. It hasn't happened, my girl, so we have to live our life as we are destined to live."

Maria's heart fluttered: she recalled her grandfather's reading and thought, "Dear Lord, I do not want to have such a destiny!"

In a few days, the broadcast brought terrible news; Italy started war against France and England. The German troops were attacking France. In the middle of June, the French government allowed fascist Germany to march into Paris. Maria cried the whole day after that news. Her Alexander was in France, occupied by Nazis.

It was strange, but the Kotyks had not yet seen the soviets at their estate. People told different stories about them. Their neighbors were evicted from their houses months ago and their properties were "nationalized." Dr. Kotyk realized that they had lost the opportunity to leave the country, and they had to be prepared for a new type of life.

The whole family had a dream of moving to Greece, where everyone had their own room in a beautiful white house on the seashore. Who could imagine such rapid changes in their life? The NKVD did not allow people to leave the country. Dr. Kotyk's friend tried to return to Canada after a visit to his parents. The authorities took away his passport and did not issue him permission for departure.

Count Kotyk prepared one wing of the guesthouse for the family to move into and another, smaller part for the office to see his patients. In the event that the soviets did not permit them to stay on the territory of the estate, the Kotyks were ready to move to grandfather's hunting lodge.

He explained to Maria, seeing her hesitation,

"The hunting lodge had been recently renovated with the addition of a big bathroom that has steam and laundry rooms. One more room with a waiting area and a separate entrance was built from the other side of the house. There we can see our patients. In other words – I tried my best, Marie, to make ready a place for our escape. Three days ago, a new bigger fire stove was constructed in the lodge, so the family could stay there during winter season without any problem with heating and cooking."

Maria leaned toward her father, thinking with appreciation, "He always takes good care of the family. We have a wonderful father. Thank God, our father is a thoughtful and kind person."

The weekdays passed by quickly. Maria and her father had busy schedules. She assisted him in surgeries in the local hospital and visited sick people at their homes. In truth, Maria was afraid to do the home visits alone. The practice grew significantly, because two other doctors successfully left the country at the right time and the Kotyks ended up consulting and treating patients from two additional areas.

The new authorities did not interfere with the medical practice and personal life of Count Kotyk, but the family lived with the feeling that every single peaceful day could be the last one in their lives. Permanent fear hung in the air.

Since the fall of Paris, Maria did not have a place to go. She prayed for her fiancé and his mother every day. The family quietly celebrated Christmas in 1941, and everyone was happy that the Christmas tree was decorated in their own home.

Most of the servants left some time before the holidays. A new political and social system quickly delivered the policy of people's equality. All the savings in the banks that belonged to the Kotyk's family were expropriated. One of the soviet slogans was, "No more landlords and servants allowed in our new democratic society!"

They proclaimed no difference between rich and poor or between educated and illiterate parts of the population. A new political power gained strength on amassing on its side those who did not want to work or study, but considered themselves devoted fighters for rightful equality in the human society. They removed all the laws of a civilized life. They destroyed a lot but did not create anything, and those who were on the top of the demonic structure knew how to use their destructive tendencies.

Only Sofia, Rosa, Ganja and coachman Ivanko stayed with the family. The children themselves cleaned their rooms. Maria helped Sofia in the kitchen on Sundays. When the snow fell, all the inhabitants of the Kotyk estate worked outside, shoveling the snow from around the house. They continued to live, trying to comply with changes in the quality of life.

It became more dangerous to travel, visiting people in different places. Maria understood what her father meant when he said that the peasants lost their meekness. It happened in March. They were on their way home after a long working day. The weather during the day was rather warm, but the temperature dropped rapidly in the second half of a day. Maria felt chilly in their light cabriolets and covered her father and herself with peasant's fur-coat that they kept it in the cabriolets for this occasion.

Maria felt sorry for her father, who had to continue working hard every day because all of his savings were expropriated by the new dictatorship. Count Kotyk was not sure of his money savings in France and Greece. Everything had been changed so rapidly that it was difficult to be sure in the existence of assets that were inherited or earned during the life. Maria could not see the correct way out of their unpredictable life circumstances. Their home was not far but tiredness put Dr. Kotyk to sleep. He dozed off and coachman Ivanko tried to ride carefully. Part of their road was going through the forest. There were no leaves on the trees, but at the same time, the forest had changed its dark gray color into hazel, demonstrating awakening from the winter sleep.

When the road turned, Ivanko slowed down and several men immediately appeared in front of the horses. The cabriolets stopped abruptly and Dr. Kotyk woke up. He saw the robbers with shotguns and asked in his usual calm manner,

"How can I help you?"

One of the men appeared near Dr. Kotyk and answered with one word,

"Money."

Dr. Kotyk made a face, as if he was surprised with the answer,

"Really? Why don't you ask the soviet bank to issue you money from my account? They took everything away and now I see that their example has affected you a lot. I am a doctor in this area since 1918. You are the first who decided to rob me. If you need our help, as a people of medicine, please come and ask for it any time. We cannot help you with anything else."

The man grabbed doctor's briefcase and stepped aside to open it. Maria noticed that somebody else came forward.

"Leave them, Orest. I recognized the doctor. He saved my wife when she could not deliver our first boy. We did not have money to pay and he knew about it ahead of time. If not for him, I don't know what could have happen to her. Do you remember me, Pan Doctor? I am Stephan from Sambir."

Dr. Kotyk replied truthfully,

"To be honest, I do not remember you and your wife. How is your wife now?"

"We have six children since then. Our family is big and I have no job. I worked in Poland before the war started. Then I came home and the militia did not want to register me and to issue me a passport. Without a passport, nobody hires me for any job."

"I am not the person, Stephan who can give you advice, but robbery is the worst choice."

The first man checked the briefcase and did not find anything interesting, so returned it back.

Maria watched her father with amazement. She realized that the robbers also saw his calmness and dignity, and maybe his peaceful behavior was the best tactic to stop their violence.

Dr. Kotyk asked Ivanko to give Stephan a chicken with which one of the doctor's patients paid him. Dr. Kotyk did not want to accept it but the woman insisted. She explained,

"Pan Doctor, I suffered due to my tooth pain for a week. You, doctor did not refuse to arrive and help me. I am sorry, but I have no money to pay. Take a chicken, please."

Dr. Kotyk explained in all honesty,

"If I give you, Stephan some money, you will share with your friends and the children will not gain anything. So take the chicken home and feed your kids. Stay blessed, Stephan and you also, gentlemen."

The robbers stepped aside and let doctor go. He did not want to discuss the unpleasant situation, closed his eyes and dozed off again.

Glory to Thee, o Lord! Glory to Thee!

Chapter 3

The unpleasant incident pushed Maria to think about the reorganization of their medical practice and not to take a risk on the roads. They heard about growth of the number of robberies on the roads and in local trains. Dr. Kotyk used to visit his patients for so many years that everyone knew him in the area and expressed respect and gratitude to him.

The new social regime pulled the changes in attitude toward doctors, landowners, the owners of the hospitals, factories, plants, banks, etc. They were stamped with two words – *capitalists* and *exploiters* that meant *social enemies*. The meanings, like *personal* or *family property* and *ownership* were altered and destroyed. A new regime changed them to *common* and *public*.

Maria suggested for Dr. Kotyk to arrange daily consulting hours in the estate office for half price. They were surprised to see three times more people at the office every day. Dr. Kotyk was proud of Maria. His daughter was great in the medical practice. She was a knowledgeable and devoted physician, as well as an enthusiastic and smart business organizer. Maria did not complain a single time about her tiredness due to the large numbers of patients during winter. Everyone liked the young doctor and with time, many women from the surrounding villages preferred Maria to examine them because they found it more comfortable.

Winter melted fast with the first warm rays of the spring sun. Maria's favorite season brought new hope: they had to wait patiently for the end of the summer and everything could be changed for the better in the Ukraine or at least the NKVD would allow her family to leave the country. Maria thought,

"Where should we go, when the Nazis are in France?"

She was making plans for the whole family to go to Greece. On Easter, April 20, 1941, the priest announced in the church that Nazi Germany together with Italy and Bulgaria occupied Greece.

On the second day of Easter, Maria had heard that somebody knocked at the gate. The family did not expect any guests. The old count was the only guest for Easter and he had arrived three days before the holiday. She called for her father. Both of them stood on the porch watching two riders coming to the house. The older rider introduced himself.

"I am Captain Nikitin. We are here to check the documents of all the people who reside in the house."

The documents were presented, checked and returned to their owners. Dr. Kotyk sent the children to the house. The officer asked,

"You are a physician, aren't you? We want you to examine a patient."

Dr. Kotyk looked at the officer.

"When do you want me to go?"

"The patient is here," the officer replied.

Dr. Kotyk invited the visitor into the office.

"I am not a patient, Dr. Kotyk."

The officer ordered the other rider to bring the patient. Dr. Kotyk opened the door of the office wondering what to expect after their visit. While washing his hands and putting on his doctor's coat, he heard noise at the door and whispering in the waiting room. Dr. Kotyk smiled when he saw his patient, a small boy about a year and a half old. Maria entered the office and greeted the people in pure Russian, with no trace of an accent. The visitors were sincerely surprised to hear their language in a land where people spoke only Ukrainian and Polish.

Maria washed her hands as well. The child's mother took the boy out of the quilt and sat him down on the examination table. The child began to cry. It was not a normal loud crying. The hoarseness did not allow the boy to inhale. Maria took his temperature.

"It is 102.6" she said.

Dr. Kotyk listened carefully to the sounds in the boy's chest. The child stopped crying and watched the doctor. The stethoscope was ticklish and the patient smiled.

"It's pneumonia."

The boy stopped smiling, as if he understood the danger of the diagnosis. Maria asked the boy's mother,

"When did he get sick?"

The young mother answered with traces of tears in her voice.

"The fever rose about three weeks ago. At the beginning, it was like a typical cold. A week ago the cough started. The last three days we did not sleep because he could not breathe."

Dr. Kotyk gave all the instructions to the parents. They wrapped the boy in his quilt and were about to leave, when Dr. Kotyk stopped them.

"I want you to understand the severity of the condition. The child needs to be hospitalized tonight. Tomorrow it could be too late. Please, do not wait until tomorrow."

The officer asked,

"To what hospital should we take him?"

"The best hospital for children is located in Lvov," Dr. Kotyk answered.

The visitors appeared surprised.

"Yesterday the doctor from the children's hospital in Lvov examined him and sent us to see you."

It was Dr. Kotyk and Maria's turn to be astonished. They could not believe that their colleagues in the children's hospital misheard the specific sounds and absence of sounds in the child's lungs. Why did they want Dr. Kotyk to be involved in the situation? Maria answered in French:

"They were not afraid of the child's death. They have been frightened with his father who represents the dictatorship. They transferred the danger and responsibility to you, Papa."

Maria invited the visitors to sit for a couple of minutes in the waiting room. She closed the door to the office so that they could discuss the ambiguity of the situation. Dr. Kotyk made the conclusion.

"The child is in critical condition. The specialists in Lvov did not want to take care of him just because they were afraid to treat the child of a Russian officer. I cannot see another reason."

"Papa, what can we do in this situation?" Maria asked.

Dr. Kotyk looked at his daughter and answered with a question,

"What do you think two physicians should do with a patient in critical condition?"

Maria looked at her father and answered,

"The case is extremely difficult, but we can try to save the boy's life. The child is not responsible for the Russian occupation, liberation, and interference in our lives. What do you think, Papa?"

At that moment, Dr. Kotyk doubted his initial recommendation to hospitalize the boy.

"Marie, do you think we can help the boy without hospitalization? Should we take a risk and leave him here? By the way, we did not ask them where they came from."

Maria opened the door and asked,

"Where are you from?"

The young mother answered,

"From Kharkov."

Everyone smiled, and Dr. Kotyk asked,

"Where do you live now?"

The officer answered,

"In Sambir."

"It's too far, Papa, for a child to go back in such weather," Maria interjected.

"Can you stay here for three days?" the doctor asked.

The visitors were surprised with the question.

The officer inquired,

"Stay where?"

"Your son will stay with his mother in the guest house of our manor."

Seeing the hesitation of the parents, Dr. Kotyk explained.

"It's very dangerous to let you go home. The crisis could occur at any moment, if not this night, then tomorrow. The illness is in a very advanced form. The boy's condition requires professional observation and twenty-four hour care."

The young mother started to cry. She was afraid to stay among strangers but at the same time, she was scared of her son's condition.

Her husband made the decision:

"They will stay but I have to go back."

At the door, the officer stopped, turned to Dr. Kotyk, and gave his hand.

"Thank you, Dr. Kotyk. I'll be here in two days."

Dr. Kotyk followed him to the porch while Maria stayed with the woman and the child at the office. The officer asked:

"Tell me the truth, Dr. Kotyk, is my boy so bad that he can die?"

"Yes. Your son is in critical condition."

Dr. Kotyk did not see the face of the officer, but felt his tension.

The officer continued.

"That's why yesterday they did not leave my boy in the hospital. They were afraid of the responsibility for his death and sent us to you. That's why they have said that you can help him."

"With God's help," Dr. Kotyk added.

Dr. Kotyk wanted to ask the father to pray for his son's health, but recalled that he was, probably a communist and they did not have faith in the Divinity.

Dr. Kotyk went back to the office and gave the boy some medications. After that, Maria showed his mother a room with two beds. The evening was quite, as the child was asleep most of the time. At eleven o'clock at night, the fever jumped up. The boy was in critical condition. Maria did not go to sleep. Instead, she assisted her father with taking the temperature, giving medications, mixtures, and preparation of cold compresses to lower the fever and to prevent the convulsions.

The fever was stubborn and did not go down a single degree. The boy fainted at three fifteen in the morning. Elena, the patient's mother, was not hysterical. She stood near his bed, biting her lips, and watched her son stuck between two worlds.

Dr. Kotyk listened to the boy's heartbeat. It was hardly detectable. He turned to Maria and asked her to bring an injection with one more medication. Maria doubted that the child could be given that shot. The doctor answered in French,

"We are losing the child anyway. It is risky, but there is no other choice, Marie. The heart requires support."

He took the syringe with the medication and said,

"Lord, bless us."

Within two minutes, the boy opened his eyes.

The doctor smiled,

"What a boy!"

The child asked for something, but the adults could not hear him, his voice was so faint. Maria showed him a jar with water. The boy stretched out his arm.

Dr. Kotyk commented,

"Your intuition was excellent, Marie. The high fever made him thirsty. He wants some water."

The mother started kissing her child. She repeated one word, "Nicky, Nicky…"

Then she turned to the doctors and concluded,

"He is not so hot anymore," and asked, "What do you think?"

"Thank God, the temperature dropped." Dr. Kotyk answered.

Maria brought a glass of water, lifted up boy's head and the child drank. The adults hoped that the boy had passed the clinical crisis.

By lunchtime, Nick asked for food. He drank some chicken broth and became sweaty and tired. Maria counted his pulse and checked the temperature. She gave him two medications, and the boy fell asleep. The young doctor listened to his lungs and commented with her beautiful smile,

"The Lord is so merciful. At night your child was dying and, thanks to God, a moment ago he asked for food."

Elena was surprised to hear that the young doctor was expressing her appreciation to God for saving the boy's life.

The young mother thought,

"They are strange people. They are well-educated physicians. They know how to treat, they have worked hard for the whole night and at the same time, they believe that God helped my Nick survive. These people are more than strange."

Dr. Kotyk entered the room and, as if reading Elena's mind, answered aloud,

"Yes, Pani (Mrs.) Elena, it can be strange for you. We do believe that God has saved your Nikolas and in this case we are here only for assistance."

In the morning of the next day, the boy felt much better. He was still weak, but his appetite returned and he wanted to be out of bed. The old Count Kotyk examined Nick and prepared four different herbal remedies for the small patient. He did not see the necessity for the boy to stay at the estate. His mother was a smart person and learned all the instructions on how to give Nick the remedies, how to feed him, and what to do in order to prevent the recurrence of the disease and complications.

The boy was very cooperative, taking remedies without resistance. Most of all, he liked the potato and honey plaster that Maria prepared for him in the evening and placed on his chest. It was comfortably warm and put the boy to sleep. Elena learned how to make it, and she promised to repeat the procedure six more times at bedtime for a week.

On the third day, Nick's father arrived. Everyone noticed that he was happy to see Nick and his wife again. The doctor's permission to take the child home was a real joy for the family. Dr. Kotyk avoided another meeting with Nick's father and left to see a patient. He felt the awkwardness of the situation because the patient's father belonged to a new authority. The most important task was fulfilled: the child was alive and the improvement was visible.

"Let the boy be healthy and blessed,"

Dr. Kotyk thought, as he left for another home visit. *Glory to Thee, O Lord! Glory to Thee!*

Chapter 4

The working days in May 1941 were very intense due to one additional job: gathering the herbs for healing remedies and delivering them to the herbarium room in the hunting lodge of the old Count. The Kotyks did not have servants at the time, except a coachman, and they had to do it by themselves every early morning for three hours. That job was always an incredibly important part of their medical practice.

Dr. Kotyk, Maria, and Rosa had to get up at four a.m. and, within half an hour, they were in their horse drawn wagon on their way to the forest. The team worked for three hours, packing the sacks with herbs and loading them onto the wagon. From there, the coachman took it to the lodge. By the time of delivery, the old count was already in the lodge, waiting for new materials for healing remedies.

The old Count had to use most of the herbs for the preparation of remedies on the day of collection, while they were juicy and fresh. One part of the raw material he juiced on the day of delivery and mixed with other ingredients and alcohol, in required proportions. The second portion of the herbs was washed, covered with gauze to prevent dusting, and hung to dry in the attic. All the bunches of herbs, jars and containers with remedies were labeled, dated, and had the information on the ingredients. The prepared remedies were taken to the basement in order to occupy their assigned places on the shelves. The temperature in the basement was low all year round, which was beneficial for preserving.

After three hours in the forest, Dr. Kotyk and Maria did their clinical work, seeing people from the surrounding towns and villages. Their usual working day lasted between seven to eight hours, but the summer herbalist job extended their workday to ten hours. By the time they went to sleep, both Kotyks were very tired.

On Saturday, June 21, 1941, the family celebrated Jennie's twelfth birthday. Count Kotyk brought her from Lvov convent school a week earlier for summer vacation. Twenty-two guests were invited to her birthday party: ten adults and twelve children. Jennie received an invitation from her Godmother to spend three weeks with Godmother's children at the Jaremcha summerhouse in the Carpathian Mountains, one of the most picturesque areas of Western Ukraine. She said that NKVD rejected their request to go to Italy, so the family decided to spend summer in the Carpathians for a change.

It was a warm day and the first table was served outside on the veranda of the house. The evening coolness sent the guests to the dining room inside the house. Sofia and Rosa volunteered to help Ganja and Martha serve Jennie's birthday party. Everyone loved Jennie, and Sofia was sure that the Universe would forgive her for working on one Saturday. The guests left at about midnight after all the interesting topics were discussed. The priest reminded the guests that he would expect to see everyone in the morning for church service.

The next morning the noise awoke Maria. Somebody knocked on the gates. She looked at the clock. It was 6:25 a.m. The Kotyks were accustomed to patients waking them up at night or early in the morning. She looked out of the window and was surprised to see priest Bogdan there. He was supposed to be in church in an hour.

"What brings him here at this time?"

Maria thought.

"Something serious has to have happened in his family."

Maria ran to the shower room and in fifteen minutes, she came downstairs in her church dress with a hat in her hand.

Two men were sitting downstairs in the living room.

"Good morning, Fr. Bogdan. Good morning, Papa."

She received the priest's blessing and kissed his hand.

Maria said with her childish smile,

"I am glad to see two fathers at the same time. What brought you, Fr. Bogdan so early? Is everything all right with you and your family?"

Dr. Kotyk interrupted,

"Marie, please sit down."

Maria followed her father's request and sat down next to Fr. Bogdan. She sensed that something unusually bad had happened.

Dr. Kotyk explained,

"Marie, German troops are in Byelorussia, Ukraine, and Russia. The bombing started everywhere. The Soviet Union is at war."

"Lord, have mercy!" Maria exclaimed.

The Nazi forces were well prepared for war, and their attacks were strong and massive. The Nazi troops quickly occupied the area. The red flags of the soviet regime were changed to white with huge Gothic black crosses. In two days, a new *ordnung* was established and massive repressions took place in many small towns and villages.

A new registration and passport control again was required in the occupied zones. Maria's dreams that everything could be settled by the end of summer sunk. She finally realized that her father and grandfather were absolutely right sending her straight back to France a couple of days after her arrival. She could only imagine how worried Alexander was with the news about the occupation of the Ukraine. None of them knew what to expect in the near future and when they could see each other again.

One morning a wounded Nazi colonel was delivered to Dr. Kotyk's clinic. The wound was in an extremely dangerous location, causing massive bleeding. The German military hospital was ten miles away, and it was obvious that the colonel could not survive the long trip. Maria's father examined the officer and concluded that immediate surgery was required. He asked Maria to assist him.

"But father, he is our enemy. How can we save the life of an enemy?" Forgetting herself, she asked that question in the presence of two German officers and three soldiers. Fortunately, they did not understand her Ukrainian.

Dr. Kotyk looked at his daughter with understanding and replied in his usual calm manner,

"You are right, mon cher. This officer is an invader and our enemy. However, the decision to become a physician, once taken in your life, carries responsibilities beyond the politics of war. Do you remember that at your graduation from medical school you have taken an oath committing you to help those who suffer and whose lives are in danger? What else was in that oath? You swore not to cause any harm. The rest we must leave to God. He will take care of other aspects. We are professional people in a medical field, and we cannot let him die without trying to help. In other words, we cannot cause harm."

Maria was washing her hands when she noticed that on that morning Martha, a new nurse, was helping with the preparations. However, Sofia was not around.

"It is strange that Martha substituted for Sofia in preparation of father's operating room and a table. And now she is delivering hot water in order to prepare the patient for surgery."

Maria looked at her father who was washing his hands thoroughly with a brush and soap. Something stopped her from asking him a question about Sofia's absence.

Maria continued thinking of Sofia's absence. Maria had not seen her in the morning.

"She was the best assistant for my father for many years. Sofia was not trained in professional nursing, but she worked as an experienced nurse. Where is she now? Why isn't she with us?"

The intensive work distracted Maria's thoughts and questions about Sofia and Rosa. In the evening, she learned about them from her father. They were Jews, and father had hidden both frightened women when the Nazis appeared at the estate. He believed that the Nazis would not discover them.

The surgery was successful and the colonel stayed in their guesthouse for a few days, recovering. Maria had to visit him twice a day to check on his progress. It was strange for a young doctor to communicate with the Nazi officer in French. He was not perfect in the French language, but her German was worse. Later, Maria met him twice for check up visits and heard how grateful he was for their surgical work.

The colonel's next visit was completely different. His wound healed and he became the burgomaster of the district. Someone informed him about Dr. Kotyk's Jewish housekeeper Sofia and her daughter Rosa. The Nazis arrived in a big truck to arrest the poor woman and her daughter.

Dr. Kotyk explained to the officer that Sofia had left with her daughter some time ago before the colonel's surgery and since then, nobody had heard anything about them. Maria could tell that the colonel did not believe her father's words. He asked again.

"When did you say she left?"

Dr. Kotyk was a person who did not lie and despised falsehood of any kind. Nonetheless, he repeated,

"Before your surgery, one or two days before, I think."

The Germans drove off.

The next day a whole detachment of soldiers with dogs appeared in front of their house again. The search lasted for hours. Sofia and Rosa were not found. Both women were well hidden in a secret room of the basement. The house was huge and nobody, except Dr. Kotyk, knew how to get into that room. There was a special system to unlock an opening in the wall to get there. There were two inconveniences: the size of the room was very small and there was no incoming fresh air. In spite of this, they were safe there.

Dr. Kotyk brought them food once a day and at different times to avoid raising the suspicions of servants. He specifically did not want his servants to talk about strange changes in their master's behavior. Although some of them had noticed that the door to the wine cellar was opened more often than usually, they associated it with the additional stress that Dr. Kotyk was under with the occupation of the Nazis.

After a few weeks, it seemed the danger had passed. Dr. Kotyk decided to allow the women to take some fresh air outside at night for half an hour or so. The fresh concentrated air invigorated the poor women. Both of them looked pale from spending days and nights in the darkness of the cellar.

Somebody noticed their short walks outside and informed the burgomaster office about their existence. Nothing could stop the fascists. They threatened to burn the house with all the inhabitants if they did not find the women. One of the young German officers hit Dr. Kotyk with a lash and, at that very moment, everyone heard a horrible, inhuman scream. The soldiers dragged both women out into the courtyard, kicking and beating them with sticks, while shouting insults.

The Germans decided to execute them in the yard for all to see, hanging them on the branches of a tree near the central fountain. Dr. Kotyk rushed to stop the execution, pleading with the colonel to show mercy and spare their lives. Everyone saw the fury in the colonel's face, but he knew that the doctor had saved his life. He steadied himself for a moment, and then announced his decision.

"Since you love these Jews so much, your daughter will be taken to the concentration camp with this young Jew," he said, motioning to Rosa.

"As for that one…"

He turned to Sofia and shot her.

At that very instant, Maria thought she heard the voice of her grandfather.

"My poor child, what you are destined to go through would be difficult for ten men. Pray hard and the Lord will save you."

Without a second to think or to say goodbye to her family, two soldiers grabbed Maria's braids and pulled her with demonic strength into the military truck.

Rosa and Maria were driven to a large barn that was located in a short distance to the railway station. The soldiers threw them into the barn, in which about three hundred Jews had been detained. On arrival, in a crude registration procedure, the newcomers were handed yellow stars of David. The Nazis forced the captured Jews to sew them visibly onto their outer garments. Maria could not stop crying. She was painfully aware that nobody could come to liberate her. There was no hope of reversing the colonel's decision. This thought stuck in her mind and kept turning over and over.

At the time of registration, the young Nazi officer promised that next morning all Jews would go to the concentration death camp in central Poland with one purpose "to take an active part in important scientific research for Reich." In other words, they would use them and their children, as raw material, for inhuman and insane scientific work and, at the end of the "experiments," all Jews were supposed to be "eliminated". It was difficult to believe that somebody could use them and their kids as an experimental material, even so, the words of the officer sounded horrifying.

Maria thought,

"It happened to me, because of my terrible destiny. Maybe I did not pray or do much in order to change it? I denied accepting my grandfather's prediction. Instead of persisting praying with three hundred bows, as my grandfather taught me in order to change the destiny, I chose the denial. Wrong! Now I am in danger and it is too late to change anything."

Maria looked at the people who were stoned in shock. Most of the arrested were sitting in silence, and only a few of them conversed with one another. People were thinking of their life; how they lived before the tragedy had happened and what they dreamed of and what they had not done yet by the moment of tragedy. Some of them tried to imagine what could happen *if* they knew earlier, or *if* they had more time for escape, packing all the family, including old parents... They were caught by hideous reality, and it was so difficult to accept, as true, that they might not be destined to hide, to run away, and to disappear. Otherwise, it would happen.

"These people are Jews, children of God. How dare the fascists persecute the God's nation? Why does God allow these horrors to happen to His people? The Creator loved His people and summoned the Jews to follow His laws and be afraid of His glorious and fearful name in case, if 'thou wilt not observe to do all the words of the law'."

Maria continued watching the people and thought,

"Did we live, being afraid of any punishment from above? We did not even think about it. We believed in God's generosity, as long as all of us were His handiwork."

Maria used to be a good student of her monastery school. She learned the Old and New Testaments well. She remembered God's warning, if people did not observe all His laws, they would be punished with different sicknesses and scattered among all people, 'from the one end of the earth even unto the other'... Among these nations they will not find any ease or rest, 'but the Lord shall give thee there a trembling heart, and failing of eyes and sorrow of mind'."

Maria asked herself,

"What was the purpose of the punishment promised by Lord? In case of disobedience, He decided to destroy great number of His people. God promised to leave few in number, 'whereas ye were as stars of heaven for multitude'; just because they would not obey the voice of the Lord their God."

It was difficult for a young mind to realize the severity of such a promise.

"I would never believe that this is God's intent to teach His people hard and inhuman way to obey God's laws. The Lord is always patient and merciful. It is Satan, who is testing strength and patience of our Creator. He found the accumulation of evil forces in Germany and created the demonic military structure that destroys God's children on Earth."

The long barn was filled with old and young, men and women, their children and tiny babies whose tears had long since dried up but were still screaming. There was no place to sit and no air to breathe.

"What am I doing here?" Maria asked herself.

She remembered that someone had mentioned that her mother's great-grandmother came from one of the Krakow Jewish families. She met her future husband at her brother's place in Krakow and fell in love with a handsome Count from the Carpathian Ukraine. There was exceptionally strong love between her mother's great-grandparents and God blessed them with three sons.

Maria looked around and felt heartrending for all the people in the barn, so frightened and hopeless. Her memory brought again the words from the Old Testament,

"And thy life shall hang in doubt before thee; and thou shalt fear day and night and shalt have none assurance of thy life."

Maria sighed deeply, "It's our mutual feeling for today – we cannot be sure of our lives."

Could any mentally healthy person believe at that time that the Nazis and their collaborators planned to annihilate more than 500,000 Ukrainian Jews in 1941 and about 700,000 in 1942? The occupants deported several hundred thousand Jews annually to different extermination camps. The world learned the places of hell on Earth for Ukrainian Jews, such as Belzec, Sobibor, Bogdanovka, Babiy Yar, Auschwitz, and many others.

How could three hundred captured people know that they were just a tiny group among one million five hundred thousand Ukrainian Jews who perished in Holocaust for the years of occupation?

A new thought entered Maria's head,

"Forgive me, my Lord for being so selfish tonight. Self-pettiness allowed me to forget about my friend. Where is Rosa?"

Maria stood up and looked around. She found her friend in the crowd and moved slowly in the direction toward her.

The poor girl sat on the floor, leaning against the wall. Maria crawled over to her and touched Rosa's hand. Rosa sat with opened eyes and did not see anybody; she was in deep shock and barely breathed. Rosa's hand was burning hot and her whole body was bruised and inflamed. Maria felt ashamed of herself.

"How could I be so selfish and forget about my friend? Poor Rosa was trampled and witnessed her mother's death just a short while ago!"

Maria sat closer to Rosa and put her hand on her shoulder. The girl looked at Maria with her huge brown eyes and burst into sobs. Maria knew that such a reaction was for better. Rosa cried, repeating two words,

"My mamma, my mamma..."

Suddenly the older man next to the girls started sobbing as well. The heat in the barn was stifling, and the air hung thick with pain and sorrow.

By morning, an eerie and heavy silence fell over the barn; even the babies stopped crying. Suddenly, the doors of the barn were flung open to reveal a railway siding. The shouting began. The guards with the dogs made the corridor from the barn to the train. The Nazis started packing the Jews into dirty cargo carriages and the full scale of the tragedy dawned on those who were too old and were unable to run fast. The guards allowed the dogs to rend old people. Some older people were summarily executed, as an example to the rest. The crowd ran fast, pulling the children by the hands and holding tightly the babies. At that moment, people completely realized their powerlessness and the long-term applications of their plight. The tragic event that took place yesterday changed their lives and the lives of the loved ones irrevocably and forever. The morning proved that no one had a chance to break the chain of unfortunate circumstances and events.

The young soldiers with huge dogs herded the prisoners into the cattle cars and slammed the doors shut. Maria noticed while running that there were passenger cars on the train as well. Finally, the train jolted into motion. At that moment, something awoke inside of Maria. She started to pray. It was a family tradition to pray as one set off on a journey in order to request the blessing of the Lord for the trip. While kneeling and praying on the floor of the dirty cattle car, Maria faced the tragedy of that unusual departure, heading towards an unknown destination.

Maria prayed, as she had not prayed in a long time. She recalled that one other time in her life she had been praying and crying for hours. It was when her mother had left them. The tragedy that Maria underwent twelve years ago was not so horrible in comparison with the current event. However, the present situation seemed many times darker and dangerous than her mother's departure. The people around her in the cattle car observed her Christian praying without interference. Only the steady noise of the train tried to deaden Maria's voice.

Maria noticed that two large fascist guards near the door were watching her worshiping. They looked surprised to see a Jew, praying in a Christian manner and kissing her crucifix. They did not interrupt her and soon both of them dozed.

The train was moving with monotonous noise, stopped occasionally for three to five minutes, and then setting off again. A man near Maria mentioned to his wife that they were probably close to the original territory of Poland.

Maria's thoughts took her to beautiful Krakow. She used to go there every year with her grandfather or sometimes the whole family. They had relatives and friends move there during the Russian revolution. They had purchased nice estates there and provided their medical practices for many years.

She remembered vividly one of their visits to Dr. Kravchuk's Krakow estate. At that time, Maria was eleven years old. She looked anemic, pale, and very skinny. Maria's appetite was poor since her mother's departure. Dr. Kravchuk could not stand seeing her sitting at the table and picking at her food. He told her stories of how he had visited his patients in the fall and winter nasty weather. In spite of the long hours he had to stay in soaking wet clothes, he had not ever gotten pneumonia.

"Do you know why?" he asked Maria.

She could not find the secret of his wellbeing and shook her head. Dr. Kravchuk answered gladly.

"I am strong and healthy because I eat well and give my body the nourishment it requires."

Being a child, Maria learned from Dr. Kravchuk that all the doctors had to be extremely strong and in good health because their work was always needed. People waited for doctors in good and bad weather, during days and nights. His excellent example encouraged Maria to recover her appetite.

The pleasant recollection put Maria to sleep. She did not know how long she slept, but she remembered her dream clearly. She saw the same dream again and again many times later. Maria dreamed of an endless field of tall green, luscious, and juicy grass. The juicy grass colored the edge of her ivory dress with a beautiful emerald color. She was wandering there for hours, trying different paths, but could not find the way home. As she grew desperate, she heard a soft voice of her Guardian Angel, saying,

"Maria, ask your Father and Mother to help you. They will definitely lend a hand in finding the right path."

When Maria woke up she remembered vividly that they were not supposed to take her home, but to help with finding the right path. Maria's dream seemed strange to her, especially at that moment. She thought about it for a while.

All of a sudden, the monotonous noise of the train was interrupted with a muffled wail followed by a massive explosion. Then they heard the wail again and another explosion, that time definitely closer to their car. The train stopped abruptly and two guards from Maria's carriage opened the doors and jumped out to check what was happening.

A chorus of terrible screams rose from the car next door. Maria and Rosa were close to the door and looked out. The car in front of them was on fire. One of the bombs had hit it and started a fire inside. People hammered against the doors, begging to be let out. The Nazi soldiers watched mercilessly, several of them were laughing loudly at every new child's and adult's heartbreaking scream. None of Nazis moved to help the ill-fated people inside of the burning car.

The planes made a circle and appeared again in the sky. The soldiers stopped laughing and ran toward the front of the train. People started to jump out of the train and Maria was pushed out, pulling Rosa with her. They ran as fast as they could away from the train and fire. They heard multiple shots and looked back, but all they could see was fire and smoke rising into the clear blue sky.

At that moment, Maria realized that they were surrounded not only by Jews but other passengers from the train. The yellow stars distinguished the girls from many other young people in the crowd. The stars were well seen in a distance. Maria stopped for a minute and tore off the yellow stars from her own blouse and Rosa's dress. Maria looked at Rosa attentively and noticed that her friend did not have obvious Jewish features in spite of her heritage. Maria had overheard something about the other passengers on the train. They were "Ukrainian volunteer workers" moving to Germany to help with the war effort.

The rest of the people continued running in unknown direction. Suddenly, the young girls heard the barking of approaching dogs dispatched by the Nazi guards. The barking of the dogs was closer and closer. The young people who ran forward stopped running when they heard that Nazis with dogs were following them. Maria and Rosa mingled with the group of volunteers. If not for the documents, no one could distinguish the girls from the workers. Maria thought,

"To work does not mean to be murdered."

Both girls were happy to be among the group of young workers. Maria believed that one hour of non-stop worshiping had changed their destiny completely and affected the destiny of other people. She whispered,

"Glory to Thee, O Lord!"

The soldiers with dogs ran fast in order to stop the people and return them back to the train. When the runaways reached the railway track again, they became witnesses of a appalling scene: all the Jewish passengers who did not run with them, had been already executed. As the group was returned to the destroyed and half-burned train, the soldiers began to pull out the Jews with yellow stars from the runaways and shoot them.

Maria's heart was pounding as the guards surveyed the group of scared to death people, searching for new victims. Rosa and Maria stood next to each other, with bowed heads, keeping deathly still while the Nazis were passing by. Maria repeated silently: *"Oh, Lord, have mercy on us and save us."* When the soldiers were satisfied with their work, they poured kerosene on the dead bodies and set them alight. The young workers were shocked at the brutality of the Nazis, many of them cried quietly.

The Nazis lined up the "volunteers" and marched to the nearest railway station along the tracks. It was approximately five miles away from the place of the train crash. At the station, Maria had a chance to see all the guards and was surprised that she had not seen two guards from their railway car who had observed her praying and who could easily recognize her. She had overheard that the second plane killed seven soldiers. Maria concluded for herself, "Those two observers must have been among killed."

At night, the group of Ukrainian workers was loaded into another train. They continued their "journey" to "a new life." Their train consisted of seven passenger cars with seats and upper and lower berths. No one was on the floor. Maria and Rosa did not find two seats in the same compartment, so Rosa occupied her seat in the middle of the car while Maria was closer to the end.

In order to satisfy the enormous demand of unskilled workers to support the war effort, the German authorities deported thousands of young Ukrainians to Germany for apprenticing and work for military industry. The German agencies provided the propaganda of "civilized, prosperous lives of Ukrainians in Germany," demonstrating the examples of the "accomplishments" of immigrants from Eastern Europe.

Faced with limited success in recruiting volunteers, the German occupants changed tactics, using persuasive methods such as threats, imprisonment, starvation, and torture. They "encouraged" the young population of the Ukraine to "volunteer" their work for the Third Reich. Everyone tried to escape "the volunteer program" but, given the improbable events of the last twenty-four hours, Maria recognized her good fortune to be one of them.

She thought,

"I must be the only one here who is so grateful to God for changing my destiny and putting me today into the 'volunteer' group. *Glory to Thee, o Lord! Glory to Thee!"*

Maria could not fall asleep on the train. Every time she closed her eyes, she saw the awful images of the day and heard the screams and pleas for mercy. Maria noticed that a girl in her compartment was also sitting restlessly, and struck up a conversation. The girl's name was Olena. Olena was in her twenties and worked as an elementary school teacher in a small Ukrainian town near Lvov. Maria visited the town many times before with her father. It was on their way to Lvov, and her friend from the convent school lived in the family estate in suburban part of that town.

Olena was also deeply troubled by the day's events and unable to fall asleep. Maria asked her,

"Where are your belongings?"

Olena replied,

"Don't you know that the first bomb hit exactly the luggage car with our belongings? By the time we got back after the chaos, the fire burned everything. We don't even have our documents anymore!" she fretted, letting out a deep sigh.

The girls were sitting in silence for a while. Then Olena asked,

"What about your belongings? Did you find anything?"

Concealing her satisfaction at the destruction of all personal documentation Maria replied,

"Oh, no. The fire burned everything to ashes. What a day!"

Maria wanted to continue the conversation with Olena about the events they witnessed during the day, but something stopped her.

"Who knows, maybe Olena is a real volunteer to serve fascist Germany and my understanding of the events could be reported immediately."

Olena gave her a knowing look and added,

"Oh, well, I guess things are not so important, Maria. At least we are alive. I cannot fall asleep after what I have seen. The moment I close my eyes, I hear again and again the voices and see those powerless people with the children and infants in the tongues of hellish fire. I would never get all those people out of my mind."

Maria could not hold her tears back and burst into sobbing, repeating the same question,

"Why did they murder them? Why did they do it to children and babies?"

Olena started to cry as well, repeating,

"Lord, have mercy. Lord, have mercy. Lord, have mercy."

Then Maria suggested praying for those who were murdered on that day.

"Remember, O Lord the souls of people executed and burned today and forgive them all their sins, voluntary and involuntary, granting them rest in Thine kingdom and make their memory to be eternal. Amen."

The girls were sitting in silence for a while and fell asleep.

In the morning, Maria noticed that just a few people in the railway car had their belongings. The passengers were sitting still on their berths under the influence of shock and fear. They could not stop thinking about the tragic events of the previous day.

At the same time, it was a chain of miracles, how the Divinity took care of Rosa and Maria. The terrible bombing did not kill them, but gave them a chance to be combined with the group of Ukrainian workers. Then the enlightening from above directed Maria to tear off the yellow stars, otherwise the Nazis would execute both girls with the rest of Jews. Later, the destruction of documents and belongings took place. In that chaos, nobody focused on Maria and Rosa. Maria was grateful to God for being merciful to both of them.

"I am grateful to Thee, my Lord, for accepting my prayers, for protecting our young lives, and not throwing us in the 'earthly hell of Nazi experiments', as we were initially promised."

The journey to Germany lasted for seven days. Maria had time for analyzing the events that happened to her during the last year and especially the previous week. She wanted to find the answer to the question that disturbed her mostly: "Why? Why did it happen to me? What did I do wrong that such a punishment was sent from above? Why did God want me to live in fear and suffering?"

There were moments when Maria wanted to scream,

"It's not fair! I haven't done anything to Thee, my Lord that I have to undergo hell."

For three days of thinking and fighting, she felt exhausted. She was in war with herself and the Divinity for putting her initially in a terrible situation without giving an explanation: Why and what was it for?

Maria felt that her mind was *boiling*.

"I can get sick just from thinking all the time and feeling offended. Offended by whom? Who offended me?"

Maria remembered her Grandfather's saying,

"Our God would never give us more than we can stand. People have to learn tolerance and humbleness."

Maria closed her eyes and recited by heart the words from Psalm 50 that she learned in her convent school,

"A sacrifice unto God is a broken spirit; a heart that is broken and humbled God will not despise..."

Maria still could not stop pitying herself. The question of *why me* was the most difficult to find the answer to. She felt emptiness inside and the endlessness of her situation. For three days, the train took her far away from home. The monotonous noise of the train slightly eased her desire to run away, to hide, and to return in her previous pre-war life. She understood that presently there was no way out, but self-pity did not let her admit it. Self-pity interrupted her sleep at night with new attacks of emotional pain and crying.

On the fourth night, Maria could not fall asleep at all. She recalled that time when her mother had left and she was not able to sleep for some time. In that case, the best medicine for stress relief was praying with her father. Presently, there was something broken inside. She sat quietly at the window, watching the changes in the landscape while the train moved further and further to the west. Maria always liked nature, but the awfulness of the situation "froze" her emotions. Only one time during the trip, she "flew away" to her pre-war life. The train was moving in the middle of the beautiful multicolored fall forest, and their beauty reminded Maria of September in Paris when she was a student at the University and Alexander used to meet her after classes. The young couple enjoyed walking along the picturesque alleys in one of the best parks in Paris, not far from Alexander's house.

Usually the weather in September was nice and the park was full of children. They walked with nannies, played hide-and-seek, and collected beautiful fall leaves of different colors and shapes while the elderly people observed the children or just sat on the benches in the pleasant sun, reading their favorite books. Maria could not help admiring the beauty and peace of the park. Every fall she mentioned to Alexander,

"Alex, I wish I could paint this scenery, it's a breathtaking one."

Maria's pleasant memories were interrupted every time with the recollection of her last visit to Creeks and the terrible events in September of 1941. There was no more peace in Europe. Destruction and death were everywhere and it looked like nobody could put an end to it. The train passed by burned forests and ruined villages and towns in Ukraine and Poland. No one collected the crops, and the full wheat and rye ears bowed to the ground.

Crossing different regions of western Ukraine, Poland, and Germany, the "volunteers" knew that they were closer and closer to the point of their destination, Frankfurt-on-Mine. Maria knew that she was arriving in an area that was not far from France, but the war built additional borders between people. They could not see each other and had to live separately from loved ones.

Maria learned to converse silently with her fiancé Alexander.

"Alex, mon cher Alex! I know that France had been occupied by Nazis. How are you there? What do you do, my darling? Do you save the lives of Nazis, as my father had taught me to do, just because we are doctors? The fascists have no right to live. They have no mercy for people, even for babies. I do believe that I was punished with my slavery for saving the colonel's life. The monster killed Sofia and broke my life without any hesitation."

Maria cried quietly, asking God in her prayers to protect her family in the Ukraine and her fiancé in France. The days were long and the nights were endless. Maria was tired of her thoughts and memories that did not allow her to relax and sleep soundly. Praying helped Maria to easier stand the long sleepless nights during her journey to Frankfurt. However, like all the rest of the passengers, she felt exhausted from staying on the train for a week and dreamed about walking on the ground, breathing fresh air, taking a shower, and changing her clothes. Maria looked forward to the last stop, but, after the horror she witnessed a week ago, she was afraid of "a new, civilized world"

On September 14, 1941 at 7:45 in the morning, the train arrived in Frankfurt-on-Mine. Frankfurt "welcomed" the volunteers with the rain and chilly weather. The newcomers were taken to plats outside the railway station, where employers were waiting to select them. All the travelers were cold and hungry. A sense of despair and indifference to their future pervaded the group.

Most of the young men were sent to work in plants and factories. Maria thought that the Germans would take women to work in families, as housekeepers, servants, and nannies. She was not afraid of those positions. Maria thought,

"I can teach children music and French. I am also good in sewing, embroidery, and knitting."

Maria smiled at her thoughts.

"It was not easy to learn all the handy things, but the nuns in my convent school had made sure of that."

Maria and Rosa were in a team of eight people chosen by a large, flabby Bauer (farmer), whose face and neck were reddened from excessive drinking. He owned two big cattle farms in the area and required workers to fulfill different duties on the farms since most of the local men had joined the war effort. The Lord took good care of Rosa. She was put to work in the house, as a servant. Maria and three other girls were sent to feed and milk the cows and clean the barns. Three men were taken to work on the construction of a new barn and to help with mowing and collecting crops.

The working day on a farm started at 4:30 in the morning and was over at 10:00 at night. Maria was petite and not used to physical labor. She was by far the weakest in the team with no experience in farming. In order to complete her daily tasks, Maria had to rise earlier and retire later than the other girls, but still she struggled. Maria was not able to finish milking in time and her tender hands could not withstand the manual labor. Within days, the skin on her fingers had cracked, bleeding continuously. In spite of persistent pain, she was afraid to complain and went on with working.

In some time, Maria discovered that she could stem the bleeding and soothe the pain by applying cream or butter to the wounds and leaving it for fifteen minutes to absorb. That natural remedy had to be applied several times per day and at bedtime.

It was Tuesday at the beginning of November and Maria had finished milking the cows. She strained the last bucket of milk and put some butter on her fingers before cleaning the barn. The pain was disturbing and she was not able to proceed with cleaning without that therapy.

Their master Gulliver used to wear a pair of very soft boots, and he enjoyed to come up and frighten the girls, knowing that nobody could hear his walking. On that morning, Gulliver appeared in the barn, walked up behind Maria, and caught her when she was healing the wounded hands. Seeing her standing idle, looking at her hands, he flew into a rage. Shouting violently in German, Gulliver grabbed Maria and threw her on the haystack in the corner of the barn. When Maria recovered her balance, she looked up and saw him, approaching slowly with a disgusting smile, as he undid his filthy trousers. Maria screamed,

"No, please, no. *O Lord, have mercy on me and save me.*"

Maria had heard from the other farmhands about his taste for inflicting violence on Polish and Ukrainian girls. She tried to scramble backwards, away from his advance. Maria whispered non-stop,

"Lord, have mercy. Lord, have mercy."

Just as he was about to catch her leg with his huge fatty hand, he tripped on his trousers that were around his knees. Losing balance, he grabbed for a pitchfork that stood against the wall to lift the haystack, but only succeeded in knocking it toward him. With nothing to support his huge body, he teetered and fell, landing on the implement and impaling himself with a terrifying roar. His roar paralyzed Maria for a minute or two. The first thought that came to her mind was: "O Lord, his family will think that I have done it to him."

Maria jumped up and ran away. She did not know in what direction she was running. She could not recall how she reached the thick and frightening forest. She cut her way through the bushes and trees with her arms, crossed the creek and ran further and further from her tormentor, his cows and barns. Maria did not know how long she was running through the forest. She scratched her arms and tore the sleeves of her wool jacket. Her heart was beating fast, as a heart of a tiny and lonely bird that had fallen out of the nest and was completely lost in a huge forest. Maria was afraid she would not find her way out before sunset and she repeated non-stop,

"Our Father, who art in the heaven, hollowed be Thy name. Thy kingdom come, Thy will be done, on earth as it is in heaven. Give us this day our daily bread, and forgive us our debts, as we forgive our debtors; and lead us not into temptation, but deliver us from the evil one."

The forest grew darker and darker, but Maria could not find the way out.

"Am I just going around in circles? *Lord, have mercy!*"

The girl was afraid of returning to Gulliver's farm. Her imagination drew horrible pictures. She was sure that the police had been already called and they were hunting for her, the murderer.

As dusk turned to night, the exhausted Maria finally saw some lights in the distance. The girl was shaking after running for so many miles through the forest and being terrified of never finding her way out. To stay in the forest at night was the worst that Maria could imagine.

"If not the farmer then wild animals could tear me apart," the poor girl thought.

The lights belonged to a small railway station. It was not even a station because there were no buildings, just a stop for local trains. Maria looked at the name of the stop but did not register it in her mind. She jumped onto the first train without any idea of its destination. Her railway car was almost empty. She hardly noticed two other women, sitting at the opposite end. Maria tried to hide herself, but it was not easy. She had no documents or money. She understood that her only hope was to find a quiet private place to work and live. She thought,

"In some time I'll let Alexander know where I am and he'll find how to save me."

Thinking of her fiancé, she felt briefly uplifted. Then the reality brought her back to earth and she smiled bitterly:

"I wonder where I can find such a quiet place."

Maria closed her eyes and began to pray silently in her heart, asking God and his Holy Mother for protection and a place to stay at night. Exhausted from her long run, she dozed off. Again she dreamt of the endless fields and heard a voice distinctly saying,

"Ask your Father and Mother to help you. They will come and show the way."

At that moment, Maria woke up, feeling as though someone had touched her shoulder. She started to pray,

"I thank Thee, O Lord for letting me run away and find the path through the wild forest. Make straight my future path; make firm my steps; guard my life through the prayers and intercessions of the glorious Theotokos and ever-Virgin Mary, and all Thy saints. Amen."

The train started to slow down, arriving to another small station. Maria stood up and went to the door. Two women were getting off and Maria followed them. It was completely dark outside. Maria noticed light coming from the lanterns in front of them. As they approached, she realized that four police officers were standing at the end of the platform. Carefully she looked for another way out, but there was none. The police officers attentively observed the three women passengers as they approached.

It was cold and one of the elderly women put on a wool hat. Maria's heart was in her throat when she covered her head with the hood of her thick woolen sweater. The old sweater belonged to one of her former co-workers, who gave it to Maria as a gift. It was two or three sizes larger, with a deformed front, and made Maria appear utterly shapeless or even pregnant. Maria decided to strike up a conversation with her fellow travelers, so she made a comment about the unusually cold evening after a nice and warm autumn day.

As the women reached the light of the lanterns, the police officers seemed distracted. They split up to check the documents of the passengers on the train. Maria looked up and thanked with her heart, *"Glory to Thee, O Lord! Glory to Thee!"*

One of the women said goodbye to them, and Maria continued her walk with the elderly one. The elderly woman asked,

"Where are you going?"

Maria did not know what to answer. She replied,

"Not far from here. I am happy to meet somebody who could accompany me at this late time."

They were going in the direction of downtown. The woman asked again about Maria's destination point. Absence of the answer and fear of a homeless night caused Maria to cry.

She made up a story. She told the elderly woman that she and her husband came to Germany from Poland in 1939. She met her husband's cousin, fell in love with him, and left her husband and his family. In a very short time, she understood that the man was not ready for a permanent relationship. Maria confessed,

"The decision to leave my husband was the biggest mistake in my life. It was me who decided to leave him and now I do not know where to go and what I should do."

The last sentence was Maria's tragic truth.

The tension of the day exploded out of Maria with a new flow of tears. Everything sounded unpretentious because Maria's life situation was really unpredictable and fearful. The woman looked at a young girl with sympathy and said,

"I am Louisa. Come with me."

The thought hit Maria like a hammer:

"I am saved again. Thank you, Lord. Today I was blessed with several miracles." Maria thanked Louisa and thought,

"Today was a really miraculous day. In the morning, I could be violently raped and killed. Later I could be lost and torn by wild animals. In the evening I could be arrested on the train or on the platform. At night, I could be homeless. I prayed, asked and knocked, as it is taught in preaching, and God blessed me with rescue. Glory to Thee, o Lord! Glory to Thee!"

Louisa's sister Martha was an owner of a big downtown bakery. Even the war did not decrease the variety of breads, pastries, cookies, rolls, and cakes in her bakery. Maria introduced herself as Marichen from Poland. From the very first day, Martha started giving Maria lessons in classic bakery. In her hands, it looked like magic art. Maria tried her best and the sisters liked Marichen and felt sorry about the "unhappy relationship" of a young girl. They were also very sympathetic that the relationship with her husband was broken forever and he married another woman.

Maria liked both sisters for being nice and generous women. They also were glad to find Maria, who was a hard worker and a very talented baker. A poor girl hoped that the nightmares "evaporated" as the morning fog with the first rays of the sun.

Maria used to get up early and became the first customer at the town farmers' market, purchasing fresh milk, sour cream, butter, and eggs for baking. The cart was heavy, but the feeling of freedom and happiness did not allow her to concentrate on its weight.

Three months passed. It was the beginning of March 1942. Maria's thoughts flew often to France, where her fiancé Alexander waited for her. He could not imagine what his bride went through. Maria recalled one day that she had told him about her grandfather's preaching for her and her friend Anastasia. Maria cried bitterly while telling him that story, and complained that since grandpa's preaching, she kept fear inside. She did not want to lose her Alexander, their happiness and joy. Alexander laughed at Maria's "funny tale." He loved Maria and it was difficult for him to imagine that something awful could happen to the woman of his dream. He promised to protect Maria with his love.

"Marie, calm down. Nothing can happen to you, mon cher. Trust me, darling, there is no any fire or frost in France that can damage you. Nothing can destroy our happy life. I shall always watch over you, defend you and keep you out of danger."

Lord, have mercy!

Chapter 5

It was a usual chilly morning in March of 1942. The rain was drizzling. The small town was just awakening from a night's sleep. Maria had finished her early shopping at the farmers' market and was returning home with a heavy cart full of dairy products. She was glad to meet Louise near the town pharmacy: Louise needed to buy some gauze for work. The elderly woman asked Maria to wait for her near the pharmacy. She wanted to go home together so they could discuss the plans of the day while walking home. When Louise returned from the pharmacy Maria understood that something terrible had happened there.

"Are you all right, Frau Louisa?"
Maria asked.

Louise turned pale, her hands were shaking when she handed a flier with Maria's picture, name, and description of the event in the village. The girl was frightened to death. The police was looking for Maria Dobrensky, "a Russian and Polish spy and dangerous killer." Louise ran away, leaving Maria with the cart stuffed with groceries.

Maria hoped that she could explain everything to those nice women. She was wrong. The sisters, being decent German citizens, called the police. The police officers waited for Maria, finishing the report.

They did not give her the opportunity to say anything in her defense. Maria was arrested and taken to the concentration camp fifty miles east of the town.

They questioned and mocked her for three days, asking for information she had never heard or known. The worst thing that happened to Maria was loss of ability to concentrate her strength and mind on praying. The feeling of endless pain, defenselessness, and lifelessness paralyzed Maria's spirit. She did not even cry. She just waited for her end. On the third day, Maria fainted, and when they checked on her in the evening, the girl was still unconscious.

On the fourth day, they stopped torturing her, and she was dragged into an old barrack that stood separately in the very corner of the camp. The soldiers threw her on the floor and someone of the inmates had mercy for Maria, giving her some water to drink. She tasted water for the first time since her arrest and could not stop drinking. The torn lips did not keep all the cold water and it was pleasant to feel it dripping on the bruised chest. Then Maria fainted again and could not track for how many days she was in a half-conscious condition. The loud screams woke her up. Her first thought was that she was again on the train with the poor Jews, surrounded by fire. In reality, their barrack was on fire.

Maria was lying on the dirty floor, watching a crowd of people near the exit door. They could not open it. Someone locked it from the outside. The poor people screamed and pushed the door, trying to escape the fire.

At last, they broke it and rushed out. Maria crawled to the exit, as well. It took some time for her to reach the doorway. She looked out and saw soldiers with dogs on the platz: they surrounded the crowd of inmates from her barrack.

Maria could not explain what happened to her at the next moment. Her next action seemed completely irrational. Out of the blue, Maria remembered that she left her sweater inside of the barrack. She crawled back in. The fire and smoke did not allow her to look up. She barely found her sweater, grabbed it, and slowly crawled out toward the exit, feeling the burning spots on her legs and arms.

What a shock she had when she reached the exit again! All of the inmates who escaped the fire were shot near the barrack. Maria could not catch her breath. She leaned on a warm wall near the exit, waiting for the roof to collapse. In expectation of her death, she closed her eyes and started to pray, hardly whispering with her cracked lips,

"O God, lose, remit, and pardon me my transgressions wherein I have sinned against Thee, whether by word, deed, or thought, voluntarily or involuntarily, consciously or unconsciously; forgive me all, for Thou art good and the Lover of mankind. Lord, have mercy! Lord, have mercy! Lord, have mercy!"

Maria was sitting for some time on the floor of the burned barrack with her eyes closed. The endless tears ran on her bruised cheeks, and she experienced a terrible burning of her face. The tears got into the deep scratches left by her torturers and irritated the skin of her face, but Maria could not stop crying. She felt her death somewhere very close and she could not escape it. The girl waited for soldiers to pull her out for execution or the roof of the barrack to collapse. When she opened her eyes, there was no fire around. Nobody went in and checked for her. The guards had finished loading the bodies of the executed inmates on the garbage carts, and had taken them to the crematorium.

Maria did not know how long she was sitting there. It was dusk, when somebody touched her shoulder. The girl looked up. A woman inmate was looking at Maria. She asked her,

"Who are you?"

"Maria," the girl whispered and fainted.

The next morning Maria found herself in another barrack. Somebody took a risk and brought her to their place. They shaved her head, due to requirement of the concentration camp, washed the wounds, gave her the inmate's clothing, and brought some her some water to drink. The next morning, Maria woke up and watched the women, lining up at the door of the barrack at a quarter to 6:00 a.m., ready to go to work.

The day was not easy for Maria. She felt high fever. By nighttime, her fever was extremely high. Maria's tortured body was inflamed, and she was unconscious most of the time. From time-to-time, she opened her eyes and asked for water. Somebody gave her some water and put a cold wet towel on her forehead. Maria's condition was critical, and the inmates did not know what to do with her. It was a lose-lose situation. The high fever could easily kill her tormented body. At the same time, there was another risk. If anybody reported her existence, the Nazis would kill her, as they planned to do it a week ago. Together with Maria, they would execute those inmates who took a risk and brought her to their barrack in order to save her life.

The fight between life and death took another week. Maria was too weak to pray, as she used to do. The longest prayer she repeated most of the time was,

"Help us, save us, have mercy on us, and keep us, O God by Thy grace."

Every time she prayed, Maria saw white light and experienced pleasant warmth inside. A miracle had happened. The inflammation in her agonizing body and high fever were slowly going down and did not make new spikes of temperature at night. Maria looked ugly. She lost a lot of weight and was extremely weak. She did not have the strength to breathe.

Currently, the girl did not know what to expect, but the recoil of her critical condition removed the initial fear of death. Maria observed herself,

"My condition is still poor: the bleeding continues, I cannot walk, inhale deeply, or even keep my eyes open, but something interesting happens within me every time I pray."

At that very moment, the light from above filled her and her persistent pain abated for some time, giving Maria the opportunity to fall asleep. The healing started. Maria praised God for taking care of her: *"Glory to Thee, O Lord! Glory to Thee!"*

It was the tenth day of Maria's stay in the barrack. While the inmates were at work, the commandant of the camp along with a group of guards arranged an inspection of the barracks. They pulled Maria out, being afraid of any infectious disease, and asked why she was not at work. Maria answered in good German about having a high fever. The language surprised the commandant. He asked,

"What is your origin?"

Maria answered,

"I am from Poland."

When he learned that she was fluent in French, Latin, Ukrainian, Polish, and German, he made an order to transfer her to the camp hospital. Maria was fluent in Russian as well, but who could take a risk in her situation and add it to the long list of the languages, as a credit?

After a one-week stay in the camp hospital, medicated treatment, and three meals per day, Maria felt much better. She was visited twice in the hospital by a camp commandant. They did not find her file, and he wanted to know everything about her, as he specified, "from being born." She watched the commandant every time, thinking of him as a polished, well-educated, and cunning monster. She prayed to the Lord not to leave her in a new dangerous situation without His Divine support.

"Dear God, be merciful and save me. I have been tortured, and I would never survive their tortures again. Give me the right answers to all the questions he plans to ask."

Maria felt sorry that she named herself again, as Maria Dobrensky. "Why? Why did I do it? They can easily identify me with this last name. The information on Maria Dobrensky they can find in any police department. What a mistake!"

She told the commandant her old story of Maria Dobrensky, who arrived with her husband from Poland in 1939, about her new love and disappointment, about her unsuccessful attempts to find her first husband, and about her stolen documents and money on a train when she had fallen asleep. Maria could not stop crying from the very first moment of her narration. The commandant did not interrupt her. He wrote down all the answers and names in order to check them later.

Maria's thoughts circled constantly in her head during the day. She was analyzing the situation,

"I had some time to live. I definitely should not mention the same name and the town I worked in. I was so weak and scared when the guards pulled me out of the barrack that could not make another story at once or at least give them my real last name. My mother's last name did not make me happy."

Maria knew that during the war, they provided the passport control all the time, and it was not a big deal to find an alibi for her imprisonment to the labor camp. She was found in the concentration camp that made the situation more complicated.

"I could easily get to the camp just due to the absence of personal documents. The absence of a passport, my accent, and my last name could be suspicious for anybody. The police could arrest me on a train when one of the patrol officers woke me up for passport control. I could forget the name of the station where they had arrested me, as I did not remember the one where I took a train on the day of my escape from the Gulliver's farm."

Maria crossed herself and prayed: *"O God, be merciful to me a sinner. Holy God, Holy Mighty, Holy Immortal, have mercy on us."*

Her thought did not give some rest: "The commandant knows that nowadays they send many people to the camps for slightly suspicious things. Usually they throw people without documents into the labor camps, but I was taken here. He asked me why they took me to the concentration camp. What explanation can I find? Who knows? I made two mistakes: I gave him the last name 'Dobrensky' and mentioned my medical education."

Maria sighed deeply and concluded, "I believe in the Lord's mercy and protection. Only Divinity can save me again."

At the end of the second interrogation, the commandant made an unexpected suggestion:

"We'll take care of your information. But for now, I want you to start working at the camp office with the translation of some materials that my secretary has prepared for you."

Maria did not want to show her joy and interest in it. It could be a test. She asked unemotionally,

"When do you want me to start?"

The commandant watched her for several minutes and answered,

"Stay in the hospital for another two or three days. The doctor mentioned that your treatment was not completed. On Tuesday go to the camp office and start your work."

He left and Maria kneeled, *"Glory to Thee, O Lord! Glory to Thee!"*

Maria's work at the office was not complicated for her. It required the knowledge of German, French, Polish, Ukrainian, and Czech. Maria was good in all of them except Czech. Within two weeks, even the translation from and into Czech was not as difficult as it had looked at the very beginning.

Maria saw that Frau Gertrude Brown watched her all the time. She reported to the commandant of the concentration camp that the translation did not keep Maria as busy as they wanted. The commandant added one more job for Maria to do. That job description required receiving daily mail, opening the envelopes and boxes, sorting the mail for other departments, and delivering it there.

A new God's miracle happened to Maria on the fifth day of fulfilling her new job. On that day, a big envelope with her personal papers was delivered to the camp. The farmer survived, and it was he, who announced the search of a 'Russian spy' Maria Kotyk. The big envelope contained Gulliver's description of Maria's "attempt to murder," his request to find the "murderer," two pictures of Maria at the farm, the police report of Maria's arrest, the reports of Frau Martha and her sister Louise, several flyers with requests to find and execute the "dangerous Russian spy and killer." Maria had to admit that the system of search and reporting in Germany was well organized even during the war.

Five minutes prior Frau Brown left for lunch, and presently, no one could watch Maria. The girl threw the papers in the fireplace and burned them without a moment of hesitation. Nobody in the camp would know that information, at least for a while. Maria was trembling and she could hardly pronounce,

"Thank you, God for giving me the opportunity to be alone in the office at the time when my records were delivered. Thank you for blessed possibility to destroy the compromising papers. I do feel myself under Your Holy protection. This means a great deal for me, it supports my hope for surviving."

Maria checked the ashes. It was dangerous to leave pieces of papers or photos there. The feeling of gratitude to the Divinity overloaded Maria and she burst into tears.

"Today could have been the last day of my life. Thank you, Lord for showing me one more miracle."

The inner tension was so strong that Maria could not stop her tears; they ran down her cheeks, dripping on the uniform and mail. Maria sorted the mail for three more departments, checking attentively for additional information about her.

Maria remembered all the instructions of Frau Brown very well.

"You, Marie, should not open the envelopes for other departments, only ours." The frightened girl was ready to endure the punishment for opening "by mistake" all the envelopes on that day. She wanted to be sure that there was no other threat for her in the rest of the mail.

Maria was still crying when Frau Brown opened the door. The commandant's secretary looked suspiciously at the inmate.

"What's wrong?" the secretary asked in her icy voice.

Maria could hardly say,

"I am sorry, I forgot and opened the envelopes that were mailed to the other departments."

Frau Brown looked at Maria and said in her condescending tone,

"I knew that you must be stupid with this simple work. You fulfilled the work of their secretaries. Next time I'll punish you. Listen carefully to my orders!"

Maria could not believe that she avoided punishment. Her heart was racing. Frau Brown looked at Maria, who was standing with a pile of mail in her hands, and commanded,

"Move it, you stupid translator! Deliver it fast and open our mail."

Maria flew out of the office. She was happy and could hardly keep smiling, but she knew well that an inmate had no right to smile. Maria tried to look serious when she opened the door of another office.

Glory to Thee, o Lord! Glory to Thee!

Chapter 6

The commandant of the camp was sitting at the office where Maria delivered the mail. He did not look at Maria. He looked, as if he was deeply involved in a conversation with an elderly man. The man was definitely neither one from camp personnel, or a military man. He wore a gray suit and light gray shirt. His silk tie reminded Maria of her father's at her engagement party. Maria put the envelopes into the mail basket and left. She did the same at the other offices on the second floor and returned quickly to Frau Brown.

Frau Brown met Maria with a question.

"So, stupid, you had opened our mail, as well, hadn't you? I thought you did it only for them. However, you should not think that doing too much is good. Learn to listen to my orders and respond exactly in the way I require from you. It was much better for me when you were occupied with your translations. I hate to repeat any instructions twice or correct anything after you."

Her voice became louder and louder. Maria could not understand what made her so angry. The girl realized,

"It's definitely not my mistake with opening the mail, so there is something else that happened while I was on mail delivery."

Frau Brown "turned off" her furious emotions, as she used to do. In a minute, she was at her desk, carefully reading the handwriting of the camp commandant with a new order that should be typed. It was short. She typed it fast and sent Maria again to all the departments to deliver it to the secretaries. Maria was happy not to stay with Frau Brown at the office. The girl thought,

"Something or somebody had made her angry and she hates me more than usual."

On her way to the other departments, Maria read the new order. It contained interesting information. The next day at 10 a.m., some inmates had to undergo "special professional testing" in the waiting room of the commandant's office. Maria's name was on the list. Maria wondered,

"Oh Lord! Maybe that made Frau Brown so distressed? 'Special professional testing'… What does it mean?"

Maria's camp personnel file contained the information on her studies in medical school. She mentioned it to the commandant and felt sorry about it. It was too easy to check and to find out that Maria Dobrensky had never been a student of a well-known school. Maria thought,

"The information on her studies could have been checked while they were arranging the "special professional testing" for us. I wish I knew what the test contained."

She tried to calm herself down with the praying, nevertheless, she could not fall sleep that night. When Maria fell asleep at around 4 a.m., she dreamed a short but interesting dream. She saw herself working in the hospital, and the hospital was in their main house in Creeks. Maria woke up and started to pray Morning prayers.

"Having risen from sleep, I strive to do Thy work, and I pray to Thee: help me at all times, in everything, and deliver me from every worldly, evil thing and every impulse of the devil, and save me, and lead me into Thine eternal kingdom..."

The next morning Frau Brown sent Maria to the commandant's office. On her way there, she tried to push away a disturbing thought of a new danger. Every time when Maria worried, she used to pray repetitively,

"Oh, my Lord, have mercy on me a sinner and save me. Amen."

With anxious thoughts and feelings, Maria pulled to open the door of the commandant's office. The big waiting room was unusually crowded. There were two officers and more than twenty prisoners there. All of the prisoners were given forms to fill out. Some of them had finished the paperwork and handed it to a slender gentleman in civilian clothing, who was sitting in a deep leather armchair in the corner of the waiting room. Maria had not even noticed him at the beginning. She thought,

"Oh, here is the stranger that I have met the day before in the personnel department when he had a conversation with the camp commandant there."

Maria was handed a general questionnaire about her medical studies and twelve professional questions that tested the level of her practical knowledge in medicine. All the questions required short and clear answers. Maria carefully read the questionnaire. The questions were not complicated, particularly for her. The girl answered them quickly because she used to be a good student and was always successful with tests and exams. The gentleman was checking the answers of the applicants, making two remarks to the officers: "Good" or "Not enough." Maria handed her papers to the examiner. He looked through all the answers and pronounced in his emotionless tone,

"Excellent. Next, please."

The officer noted something on his paper and ordered Maria to pack and to be on the camp platz ready to leave in fifteen minutes. It was easy to pack when there was nothing to pack. She put in her rucksack a second uniform, underclothes, a pair of summer shoes, and a prayer book. She was not able to get rid of one thought.

"Where should I go this time? What should I expect there?"

On her way to the camp plaza, she started to pray and sensed warmth inside - exactly that warmth that she had experienced several times before when the train with all their documents was bombed and burned, and nobody knew who they were and what their final destination was. It was the same warmth that Maria sensed in the camp barrack where she was in critical condition and when the Holy Spirit was healing her.

"Thank you, Lord! I am so grateful to Thee."

On the plaza, there was a group of six inmates: four men and two women. They stood in silence, waiting for new orders. There were no soldiers with dogs around them. An officer brought and handed the gentleman in a gray civil coat the identification documents of the inmates with photos, numbers, and necessary personal information. The gentleman signed the release form. Everything was done in accordance with the regulations.

The officer turned to the inmates and ordered them to get onto a small bus, and to take their seats. Then he jumped into the bus, looked at them and ordered the inmates to sit separately – one on a seat. In a couple of minutes, the bus was checked at the gate and rode off, taking people in an unknown direction. Maria sat in the back of the bus and had an opportunity to observe her fellow-passengers. She found only one inmate that she had met before. He worked for the camp hospital. There were thousands of prisoners in their camp and it was difficult to meet the rest of the passengers earlier. The inmates looked tense, tired, pale, and skinny. It seemed that there was nothing in the world that could cheer them up. Maria did not know anything about her new destination, but she felt that it was sent from Above. She closed her eyes praising God, *"Glory to Thee, O Lord! Glory to Thee!"*

The small bus rode alongside the groves and fields. They were the shade of bright green color, as it usually was at the beginning of summer. Maria enjoyed this time at home in the Ukraine. Home, it was so far away and seemed absolutely unreachable at the moment. She did not know in what direction the bus was taking them. The obscurity did not let her relax and enjoy the beauty of the summer nature.

Maria thought,

"The last time after Gulliver's farm I took the train to the north. Why north? It was the only train staying with the opened doors at the railway platform. Where do they take us now?"

Then she shook her head.

"It does not matter, where I go. I wish to be just further from the camp. *Help us, save us, have mercy on us, and keep us, O Lord by Thy grace.*"

Maria pulled her cross out, kissed it and prayed,

"*O good Mother of the Good King, most pure and blessed Theotokos Mary, do thou pour out the mercy of thy Son and our God upon my passionate soul, and by thine intercessions, guide me unto good works, that I may pass the remaining time of my life without blemish, and attain paradise through thee, O Virgin Theotokos, who alone art pure and blessed. Amen.*"

Worshipping made Maria calmer and she dozed. She dreamed about her work at a new hospital. Maria saw operating rooms, crispy white uniforms, a lot of patients and their treatments after surgeries, bandaging the wounds, putting the arms or legs in a plaster cast, changing the dressings, applying the compresses with different medications, and Grandfather's herbal remedies. She saw her grandpa explaining to her how to use different remedies for different cases.

Then she saw crutches everywhere in the hospital. It seemed to her that she heard the bumping of multiple crutches against the floors. She woke up smiling. She allowed herself to smile for the first time after a long period of fear and nervous tension.

Maria thought,

"What a dream! But everything looked so real! The funniest was applying the compresses with grandfather's remedies."

Maria looked around, observing her fellow travelers. They were asleep, and she noticed that the tension in their faces and bodies was slightly released. Their age were somewhere between thirty and thirty-five. Maria was the youngest among them. In a month, she would be 23. For her twenty–three years, she had been through a lot.

Maria closed her eyes and her memory took her through the most dramatic and significant moments of her life: mother's departure, grandfather's prophesying, school years in France, her love for Alexander and their engagement party, arrival in the Ukraine after her graduation, double occupation of her native land, and her "journey" with the devastated Jews. It seemed to her that she could hear again and again their voices, asking for mercy. Then her slavery at Gulliver's farm and escape into nowhere. She recalled her arrest and torture in the concentration camp and God's miracles that happened to her in the fatal situations.

Maria shook her head and stopped the "horror movie" with the thought,

"I believe in Thee, my Lord, and the miracles Thee created for me. I am twenty-three and I want to live and to serve Thee to the end of my life."

Maria was happy that she took a seat at the back of the bus and nobody could see tears in her eyes. It was her solemn oath, sworn to God. In her twenty-three years, Maria knew well that there was no power that could force her to break that oath.

It was quiet on the bus. The fellow travelers slept soundly. The gentleman in gray dozed on the front seat. Maria's thoughts flew away to Paris, where Alexander was waiting for her. She thought,

"He'll go crazy when he learns everything that has happened to his bride. He loves me so much, but even his love has not protected me as he promised one day. Why?"

Maria sighed and answered to herself,

"Everything has happened because I did not listen to him and left for the Ukraine after my graduation."

Maria's desire to see her Alexander was strong. She wanted to look into his beautiful blue eyes, touch his hair, listen to his voice, and tell him her long story about two years of life without him.

"Alex, these two years were the most difficult in my life. If I saw it some time ago as a nightmare, I would never apply it to myself. I was so foolish, thinking that God punished people for their dead sins or crime. No, Alex, I was wrong. I did not do anything against God or people. I just got into the wrong place at the wrong time or maybe, that was my destiny. You promised to protect me, but I was far away from you, darling. I miss you so much. I love you and my love was not diminished a bit even with the horrors of war."

Maria opened her eyes and was sitting for some time, watching the green fields they were passing. Her thoughts were not with the fields. She was still involved in her "conversation" with her fiancé Alexander,

"Mon cher Alex, I believe that one day with God's help we'll find each other and will cherish every moment of our mutual life."

She looked again at her fellow travelers. Maria was amazed how peaceful they looked while sleeping soundly. She thought,

"It looks like they know everything already about their journey and what is expected at the final point of destination. Now I know that people get accustomed to every day danger and with time they become rather indifferent to the fearful situations."

It was late afternoon when the bus made a turn from the highway to a local road through the forest. The road was so narrow that it was difficult to look out of the window. The branches of the trees scratched the roof of the bus and brushed the windows.

Maria noticed,

"There is no traffic on this road. The cars are probably the only vehicles here that do not touch the trees."

In about an hour, the bus stopped at the heavy gates of the country estate, hidden deeply in the woods. There was a sign on the gates that read "Linden Hospital." The hospital was a beautiful structure, consisting of a two-storied central building and two one-storied long wings. The day was warm and the wounded people were sitting on the benches and in wheelchairs around the central fountain.

Maria thought,

"The fountain is not as beautiful as in our estate. And the gates are too heavy and plain."

Those thoughts made her angry with herself.

"What nonsense I am thinking about! What can I compare? There is no more life with fountains and gates. It does not exist in reality any longer."

The pre-war life was so beautiful and peaceful in comparison with Maria's present existence that she admitted,

"Maybe it belonged to a beautiful fairy tale."

All of a sudden, Maria's thoughts were interrupted by a voice from her dream,

"Remember, you must be one of them: watchful, cautious, strong, and hard-working. From now on you have to concentrate all your thoughts, feelings, knowledge, and strength on surviving and nothing else."

The bus stopped in front of the building and the inmates sat quietly, waiting for further instructions.

Maria confessed,

"If the horrific war was not the reason for my stay here, nobody could force me to concentrate my entire self on two things only: life and death. I do not want to think about death in my twenty–three years. Every day danger, unbearable pain, and fear brought up that thought all the time."

She looked up and answered,

"I hear Thee, my Lord, and I promise that I'll do my best with Thy Holy blessing. I do not want to die. I want to see my family, be happy with my Alex, and to help people in restoring their health."

Maria remembered that all the tragic events in 1941 made her disturbed and depressed. Self-pity, absence of a visible exit from the vicious cycle, and inability to change anything in order to break the cycle once and forever affected Maria's mind and spirit. Recalling that time when she could not leave for France, the occupation of France by Nazis, and the occupation of western Ukraine initially by the communist Soviet Union and later by fascist Germany overloaded Maria with emotional pain.

"Thank God, I have learned to rely on Divinity that always saved me in miraculous ways. I discovered that my physical and emotional sufferings made me forgiven, stronger and saved by God."

Living in captivity made Maria cautious to the point of suspicion. Normally, she was open and trusted people around her. Due to her dangerous life, she learned to be quiet and circumspect. She was silent most of the time and talked when she was asked to. Maria was a victim or witness of inhuman cruelty caused by humans and learned well that only Divine forces could always be trustworthy. She had no doubt that anybody else except God could keep her alive in the situations she went through.

The bus driver left the bus with the inmates near the front entrance of the hospital. The inmates waited there for new orders for forty minutes. Maria again noticed tension in faces of her fellow-travelers.

She did not want to let a new wave of fear to cover her and started praying silently,

"O, my Lord, have mercy on us and do not send us back to the camp. *Help us, save us, have mercy on us, and keep us, O Lord by Thy grace.*"

She learned well that people could ask for anything, but only God would find better ways for answering their prayers. Two years ago, she considered herself a decision maker. It was so simple to make decisions in her pre-war life. The hardship of war and inability to change the circumstances taught Maria a new lesson on how a human should rely on God. The presence of the Divinity in her everyday life made the miracles possible.

Maria did not want to sit in tension and wait for someone to come and take them in. She closed her eyes and a bright memory took her into her childhood. When Maria was twelve, her Grandfather taught her the introductive lesson about God's presence in everyone and everywhere. It was not easy to understand that phenomenon with a child's mind. The girl could not see Him. In accordance with her Grandpa, God stayed with her, her Dad, her brothers, small sister Jennie, all the servants, and at the same time with their mother, who left them and lived far away in Canada with her new children. It was God's miraculous simultaneous presence.

Grandfather explained how it could be possible,

"Our Father creates everyone with love and blesses all of us with souls. The human souls are invisibly connected with God, our Creator. Through souls, our Father Almighty receives all the information about us: our lives, needs, thoughts, and deeds. Nothing can be covered or hidden."

Maria asked,

"Grandpa, what happens to people if they do something wrong and our Father learns it? Does He punish them?"

The voice of a small girl was trembling. The old count looked at Maria attentively and answered in his straight manner,

"Marie, our Father is patient. He tries not to punish us at once, giving us some time for thinking about our wrong deed. He expects from us the repentance and a strong desire to correct our mistake. We need sincerely ask Him for forgiveness because He is the only One who can forgive us and bless us for another chance in finding the right path to happiness, success, and prosperity."

For a while, Maria was observing her grandfather with amazement. He knew so much about God! Then the girl asked a question that was the most important for a child at that time.

"What about our Maman? If she does not repent, will God punish her? Grand-papa, in what way He will punish her? I do not want Him to punish my Maman."

Count Kotyk Sr. looked at his granddaughter with sympathy and replied with bitterness in his voice,

"You can pray for your mother, Marie. You can ask God to be merciful to her."

Currently, Maria had her own experience with the presence of God. He blessed her with showing His apparition in different ways: in dreams, Angel's voice, white light and pleasant warmth. She absorbed the knowledge with her soul, heart, and mind. She became compelling and was not terrified so easily because she believed in protection from Above. Maria whispered, *"Glory to Thee, O Lord! Now and ever and for ages of ages. Amen."*

Finally, the driver returned and drove the bus to the freight entrance. The officer appeared at the front door of the bus and ordered the passengers to line up near the entrance to the building. The officer brought the inmates all of the instructions. They were given one hour to take shower, put on their new uniforms and have dinner. In an hour, they had to be ready to meet the chief-of-staff and medical personnel of the Linden hospital.

The officer ordered to bring all the belongings and the guards took them away. They supplied the inmates with uniforms, towels, and shoes and sent them to take shower. After shower, the guards took them to their rooms. In the rooms, the inmates found boxes of civilian clothing with a name on each box. So besides a new, crispy, white medical uniform (exactly from Maria's dream), they were given additional clothing. It was second-hand, but in good condition. Maria received a brown woolen dress with a white collar and cuffs, a black skirt, two blouses, a gray suit, a thick woolen sweater, a warm coat for cold seasons, a rather elegant mackintosh for warmer seasons, two pairs of shoes, and two summer dresses. Everything was one size too large except the shoes, but in general, it looked good.

Maria thought,

"What is it? Is it a kind of liberation or a new type of slavery? Whatever it is, I remember the instruction of the voice: I have to become one of them."

All the answers were given in an hour. It was definitely not a release because the inmates were forbidden to write or receive mail, to be involved in conversations with patients and medical personnel, to make contact with the local people, and to leave the territory without special authorization. The authority of the hospital forbade writing journals. They also forbade having any kind of relationship with the personnel or patients. In the event an inmate did not follow the orders or regulations of the Linden Hospital or transgress them even partially, he or she would be summarily executed. In order to prove the severity of the requirements, the inmates were demonstrated a gibbet with two nooses in the center of the backyard of a beautiful mansion.

The next day the inmates were scheduled to work 12-hour shifts at the hospital with two 30-minute breaks. Maria was sent to the operating room for three days a week and three and a half other days she was assigned to work in a dressing room, changing the bandages and compresses with medications. On Sundays, Maria was given half a day off, and she was allowed to attend the church services in the nearest town with a few people from the hospital.

Maria could not wait for Sunday morning. She looked gorgeous in her gray suit and black shoes.

"It's a pity that I do not have a hat and a purse,"

Maria whispered, looking in the mirror. That feminine thought made her smile. She went downstairs and saw a line of people receiving the church money. They walked for a mile in silence and took the local train to the nearest town.

The church service started at 9 o'clock. Maria always remembered her first day in that small German Catholic Kirche (church) in a small town near Erfurt. The train arrived half an hour earlier and there were only a few people in the church. Maria opened the door and entered. The Divine scent made her dizzy. She kneeled and burst into tears.

"My God! What a joy to be here, at Your place!"

She looked at the icon of Holy Mary and happiness filled her heart.

"Oh, dearest Mother of God, I am so grateful for your merciful support. Am I rescued? Am I saved? Is this the end of my suffering? I'll do anything You want me to do. Will it save my life?"

For the first time since Maria had been taken from her home, she was crying with relief and joy. She wanted to believe in her happy future, but could not pick up any sign from above. There was no warmth, light, or voice. Maria continued praying with hope... *"Glory to Thee, O God! Glory to Thee!"*

Chapter 7

It was a hot August in 1942. There was a lot of work at the Linden Hospital. The hospital specialized in admission of the wounded officers of the Luftwaffe - Aviation. Flying over the Russian troops and cities and bombing the targets became more dangerous. Maria stood for long hours in the operating room. The days seemed to be endless. Sometimes they had to operate at night.

Slavery taught Maria to be silent. Inmates did not speak a word in the dining room when they were sitting at the separate table from medical personnel. The "informers" were everywhere, and the administration of the hospital received all the reports and took the required steps. One of the wounded officers brought a bucket of flowers for a young maid, and they talked for five minutes in front of the house. She was executed in an hour for not following the orders. Could anybody think about human relationships, friendships, or just keeping up the conversation with a patient or another member of the medical team after that execution?

One day Maria had heard the Russian language on the unloading dock. The transport brought some Russian officers. Two of them were in critical condition. They were wounded several days ago, and no one took care of their wounds. The third one had severe damage to his right leg with several bone fractures. He did not faint, unlike two other officers, but could barely stand the excruciating pain.

The chief-of-staff of the surgical department decided to provide night surgeries. One of the Russian officers died on the operating table, and another one was also close to passing into another world due to the severity of his wounds and internal bleeding. His condition was dangerous. The officer lost a lot of blood. The blood transfusions had little effect.

Maria wondered, "Why do the Germans try to save them?"

They were enemies and a miracle happened... By the end of the day the condition of the second Russian officer deteriorated and after another examination, two surgeons decided to repeat the surgery and find the cause of the internal bleeding. The last time they had removed a bullet from the right lung, but the worsened condition required new prompt actions.

Maria was sent to prepare the operating room, and in twenty minutes, they started the surgery. At that time, the chief surgeon, Dr. Kraus, quickly found the additional cause of the officer's internal bleeding. Two surgeons and Maria worked with good professional speed and Maria prayed silently, asking God to keep the patient in stable condition during the second surgery.

The young officer survived the surgical procedure, but it took an hour to recover after it. They took him back to his room near the nursing station. The fever rose. The chief physician put a nurse in his room. Barbara was a

Polish woman, who arrived from the camp together with Maria. She was assigned to take care of both Russian officers because she could understand their language.

At night, Maria had a dream. Her Alexander arrived at the Linden Hospital. The only thing she did not remember clearly, if he was a patient or a visitor. All the rest of the details Maria remembered very well, even the smell of his favorite cologne. Maria's sweet morning dream was interrupted with a noise. A transport delivered new patients to the hospital. It was still a cruel war and there was no time for the girl's sweet dreams.

Maria got up, and standing in front of the window, asked God to send her that dream again, a pleasant dream about her Alex. She believed that one day with God's help he would find his bride. From the very beginning of their relationship, Maria sensed him as a noble prince from a favorite fairy tale who was destined to save her. The concealed expectations and beliefs gave Maria the strength to live.

On the workdays Maria followed a usual routine - taking a shower, morning prayers, small breakfast, consisting of a cup of coffee or tea with butterbrot (a sandwich),

and rushing off to work. On that day, everything was shifted, as her sweet dream about Alexander's visit to the Linden Hospital. Some patients, including the Russian officer, were in critical condition and required special attention. The physicians had to provide personal nursing care for a day or two in order to lead them through the crisis.

Maria was ordered to come downstairs one hour earlier. They assigned her to take care of the Russian officer who was very weak after the second surgery. He looked very pale and was unconscious most of the time. His fever was extremely high and did not diminish over the last twenty-four hours. He talked deliriously and tried to get up. Maria was sitting next to his bed, changing the towels with cold water on his forehead. The second Russian officer was much better and tried to talk to her. Maria pretended that she did not understand the language, and he was just observing her work until he fell asleep.

Usually the personnel did not know the names of their patients. A nurse brought the medications for both of them, and Maria read the name on one envelope: Alexander Stern. It was the name of the pilot after the second surgery.

The day was very difficult. The chief physician and a surgeon examined Alexander twice during the day and were not satisfied with their findings. When Maria's shift was over, she noticed that she did not want to go upstairs. She worried how Alexander could survive another night.

Maria prayed for him. She was not able to find an answer for her question,

"Why? Why am I involved emotionally in this case? He is nobody to me." Probably his Russian facial features, the light color of his wavy hair, and the same name reminded Maria of her fiancé. The final answer was not found, but Maria continued praying, asking God to keep him alive and to heal him.

A new nursing shift started their work hours ago, but no one was sent to substitute for Maria. She was very tired. It was not even the right word to describe her condition: Maria was exhausted. She did not have enough air in the room, and she opened the window slightly. A flow of fresh, cool air came into the stuffy room. Maria enjoyed the freshness of the air:

"Why didn't I open it earlier?" Maria asked herself.

Alexander moaned and pronounced someone's name. Then he called out for his mother. In a couple of minutes he sat up in his bed, opened his eyes, looked at Maria attentively, as if he was trying to recognize the person, and fainted again, talking deliriously. There were hours and hours of fighting between life and death. Maria continued her prayers. She asked the Lord for help. She begged Holy Mother Maria to protect Alexander from further complications. She changed the towels with cold water on his forehead every fifteen to twenty minutes, but the fever made them hot and dry again. He stopped fighting with somebody or something around 2 a.m. and fell asleep, breathing calmly. Maria was completely drained, and dozed off.

It was chilly in the room when she woke up. She closed the window and stayed there praying to Holy Mary. It was a quarter to three. She remembered from her childhood that every early morning, the Mother of God flew around the world, watching people. When children were up, they prayed one of their first prayers:

"O Theotokos and Virgin, rejoice, Mary, full of grace, the Lord is with thee; blessed art thou among

women, and blessed is the Fruit of thy womb, for thou hast borne the Savior of our souls."

Maria checked on the patients. Both of them slept soundly. The nurse came in with the injections and took their temperatures. There was no high fever. Maria asked for the doctor's permission to leave. He was surprised that no one substituted for her at 11 p.m. She had one hour to sleep, but she was glad to be there and to help Alexander Stern go through an unbelievably difficult struggle for life.

Thank God, the next day was Sunday. Maria could sleep forty-five minutes longer. She put on her Sunday dress, a hat, and a pair of new shoes that one of the female doctors gave her as a birthday gift, certainly with the permission of the hospital administration. She looked tired but ready to go to church. Maria wanted to thank the Lord for His saving of Captain Stern's life and to light the candles for Alexander's healing.

Maria needed to receive the church money and she came down to the first floor. The doctor from the night shift was giving the report to the chief-of-staff. Maria heard how he mentioned that the condition of the Russian officer was stable. Then he saw Maria picking up the envelope with the Sunday money and asked her to come up. It was not a command. When Maria approached, he explained to the chief-of-staff that he felt sorry for Maria that she was not substituted for nearly 24 hours. Then he added, smiling,

"Today I insist in giving Freuline (Ms.) Maria one more Sunday envelope for pastry and chocolate." Maria thanked them and left.

In the church, she lit the candles and praised the Lord and Virgin Mary for their care of the Russian officer. The young girl could not find the explanation why she did all that, but she continued asking the Lord to help Alexander, to heal his wounds, and to prevent any complications.

The new week was very difficult for Maria. She could not see Alexander Stern and she did not know anything about him. There were moments when it seemed to Maria that she was ready to die but to see him, to be with him, to hear his voice, and to touch his wavy hair.

The dreams did not let Maria rest at night. They were so different. Some of them she could not remember at the moment she woke up, but another did not "evaporate" from her mind for the whole day. It looked like there was no connection between her dreams and the exciting events. Nevertheless, there was something precarious in all her dreams and it kept Maria alert.

Her dreams and thoughts did not bring any enjoyment. She experienced frequent suffocation at night, as if she was under tons of weight. Maria sensed that it was not her human intuition, but her Angel who stopped her every time when she was ready to run and meet Alexander Stern, talk to him, and declare in Russian about her feelings. It was her Guardian Angel, who put her in prayers and taught her to bring her problems to God.

Maria thought that her prayers were answered when in two weeks she saw Alexander through a window of a dressing room. The Russian officer walked slowly around the fountain. Maria leaned out of the window, observing him. He was still weak and pale, and he had a problem with shortness of breath while walking.

"Oh Lord, be merciful and heal him."

Since that day, she saw him three times per week when she worked with changing the bandages. The young man became noticeably stronger with every week.

"Thank You, God, thank you, Holy Mary for this miracle."

Maria saw him two more times in the dining room. His wavy hair grew and looked nice. He had calm manners and a pleasant voice. He did not remember anything from that horrible night.

It was so unusual for Maria to have a chance to think about personal things during the day. One morning while she was waiting for the surgeons to come, Maria thought about her strange attraction to Russian aviator. Presently, she got stuck with something that she knew was not her and *pure enough*, but she was not able to resolve the problem.

"*My Lord, please compass me! Remit, pardon, forgive, O God, our offences, both voluntary and involuntary, in word and deed, in knowledge and ignorance, by day and by night, in mind and thought; forgive us all things, for Thou art good and the lover of mankind. Amen.*"

Now Maria could better understand the situation with her Maman. Her poor mother met someone who attracted her, as a magnet. He pulled her out of her family, as a tornado, and dropped her off on another continent. Anna forgot about the existence of her husband and children, about eleven years of her family life, respect and love, consideration and kindness, obligations and responsibilities. The evil tornado splintered her spirit, mind and soul into tiny pieces, and Anna lost the ability to sense of inevitable God's punishment for her sins.

"I feel sorry for you, Maman. Now I know that strong feelings exist, but at that time when I was ten, it was so confusing that a stranger became the most important person in your life. You did not want to put the situation in the hands of the Savior and wait for His blessing or cancellation. You followed your choice. But why didn't God stop you as He stopped me several times?"

Once Maria had a chance to work in a dressing room alone and Alexander came for changing the bandages. Maria mentioned that every Sunday she lit the candles for his health in the local church. Being pleasantly surprised, the officer looked at her with real appreciation and said in his pleasant voice,

"Spasibo" – "Thank you."

The workdays flew by fast. The seasons of the year changed in their annual cycle, but the war seemed affected even the speed of the seasons changes. They were moving faster as well. The German army was stopped in Russia and had to retreat on many fronts. The Linden Hospital admitted more and more wounded officers of the Luftwaffe. The chief-of-staff brought a new team of medical personnel from the concentration camp, and a third operating room was added to the surgical block. The Ordnung (order) became stricter. Two more workers of the hospital had been recently executed in the backyard. Fewer people were allowed to go to the church services on Sundays. Maria was happy that the administration of the hospital did not cancel her trips to the church.

One Sunday, Maria rushed to the train station to catch a train to the church. She was pleasantly surprised to see Alexander on the platform. He was sitting on a bench, waiting for a train. He recognized Maria from a distance and stood up politely to greet her. The girl was glad to meet him outside of the hospital. Captain Stern smiled and started the conversation:

"Good morning, Fräulein Marichen. Will you show me your small German church, where you lit the candles for my health?"

"With pleasure, Herr officer."

The train arrived and the young people got into the same carriage. It seemed to Maria that her heart was singing and dancing, ready to fly away. She looked around and was happy not see anybody else from the hospital.

Captain Stern asked in German:

"Where are you from?"

"I am sorry, but I am not allowed to talk about myself."

"Excuse me, please I didn't know your rules. I am from the republic of Volga Germans. My father is from

German family and my mother is half Russian and half German."

"I feel sorry, but I did not even know anything about the existence of such a republic in Russia," Maria replied honestly.

They went to the second compartment and took their seats from both sides of the table, facing each other.

"In the middle ages merchants, craftsmen, farmers, master builders, architects, physicians, and others arrived from Germany to Russia. The Russian tsar Peter the Great provided Europeanization of Russia and brought many German professionals into his empire. His successors also filled important diplomatic and army positions with Germans."

Maria was fascinated about the facts of history with which she had not been familiar.

"I did not know much about those facts. What happened later?"

Alexander Stern answered:

"In 1763 Catherine II issued a manifesto in which she allowed the foreigners to settle and work or farm in Russia. The Germans were permitted free exercise of their religion. The foreign colonists were freemen in contrast to Russian peasants."

Maria found the conversation very interesting and wanted to know more about the history of Germans in Russia.

Captain Stern continued:

"The system of inheritance when the youngest son inherited the land or business, as well as the privilege in buying new lands were factors which led to founding in the 19th century of numerous daughter German colonies."

"In what parts of Russia were they founded?"

"The daughter colonies were founded in the Volga and Black Sea regions, in the northern Caucasus, in the Urals, in Siberia, Kazakhstan and central Asia. The colonies were strictly divided along religious lines: Lutheran, Catholic, Baptist, Mennonite and others."

Maria was excited: "It's so interesting. I wish we learned it in our history lessons. I could not imagine that there were so many Germans in Russia and the Ukraine. What happened with Russian Germans in XIX-XX centuries?"

Captain Stern smiled bitterly and answered,

"Do not think that the Germans sustained the privileges forever? Native Russians envied their economic success and found them a foreign body that could be eventually become dangerous and in 1871the special privileges were cancelled."

"Did all of them continue to live in Russia?"

"No, Freuline Marichen. In 1912 approximately 300,000 Germans emigrated from Russia to North and South America."

"How did they come along with red dictatorship in Russia?"

"In fall of 1929 about 14,000 German farmers with their families came to Moscow with their intention to emigrate. After long negotiations Germany finally accepted 5,000 people, but only for transit overseas."

"What happened to the rest of the families, who went to Moscow?"

"The others were returned to nowhere and my parents were among them."

"What happened to the Germans, I mean Russian Germans at the beginning of this war?"

"The Volga-German Republic was dissolved in 1941. My parents together with other German families from Russia were lucky to arrive to southern Germany in 1942."

The train arrived to a small town. They walked in silence to the church, feeling that something mutual bound them together. What was it? None of them could answer the question.

Captain Stern and Maria entered the tiny holy place and she started to pray. She asked God to forgive her excessive concern about a stranger. The girl did not know from where that obsession had come but felt that she was not able to get rid of it. She asked Mother of God to help and, if it was dangerous, to protect her.

That Sunday Maria did not hear the prayers of the priest. It was so clear: she was involved in something unusually strong. She loved her fiancé with unconditional and beautiful love. She missed him very much. At the same time, she was deeply involved with the enemy, the officer of a hostile army.

Different thoughts flashed in Maria's mind,

"It is bad what I feel about him. He does not know who I am, from where I am, who my family is. I must forget him forever. I have my Alexander... Dear God, forgive me! Help me to get rid of this delusion, please! Grow hatred in my heart, if it is necessary, but cleanse me from this obsession forever."

On their way back from the church, she explained to Alexander Stern,

"I am sorry, but we are not allowed to have any friendly relationship with patients of the hospital." Then she suggested him, "Walk slowly and enjoy the nature of the forest and this nice weather."

He appeared to understand Maria, but looked upset. Maria knew he was still weak and could not walk fast. As for her, she ran away. On her way to the hospital, Maria thought about human choices.

It was difficult for a young woman to understand why it happened to so many people, and why those nice and smart people were not able to define the wrong choices from the very beginning. She learned it not only by the example of her poor mother, but with some other cases that occurred with her fellow students.

All of a sudden, Maria's memory refreshed the words of her grandfather when their mother departed. He explained to Maria's inconsolable father,

"Lukian, Satan was always strong, and he spread his demons among people." The girl remembered clearly the warning intonations in her Grandfather's voice,

"The demons watch us and "try" people in different ways with the only purpose: to win the fight with God. They make people unhappy, depressed, disturbed, angry, sick, and the worst of all - offended with our Creator because He did not protect them. None of us wants to see this battle as our test. It may be the most important test in our life. The demons look for strong personalities, happy and talented people. They "work" hard to change everything in our lives. Their victory in the fight with a weak person does not bring them a big reward from Satan. When they capture a decent, pure, godly person and twist the person's heart and mind, they receive a bigger reward. I want you, my son, to remember that our Lord is always for happiness and love, but we have to ask Him every day to protect our love and happiness from the evil forces. People need to learn to be cautious and always ask God, as a wise father, to approve their choices."

On that day, the girl did not notice the beauty of nature as she used to enjoy every Sunday. She ran faster and faster. She was running away from something that was not right. Her heart was racing in her chest. She could sense the painful heartbeat in her throat. She was running away from her delusion.

Maria opened the door of the room and was disappointed. Her roommate Barbara, a Polish nurse, was there. Maria kneeled in the corner, burst into sobbing, praying in a low but emotional voice.

"God is our refuge and strength, an ever present help in trouble..."

Barbara gave Maria a puzzled look and left. Maria cried in repentance, asking for forgiveness.

"Blessed is he whose transgressions are forgiven, whose sins are covered. I acknowledged my sin to you and did not cover up my iniquity. I said, 'I will confess

my transgressions to the Lord and you forgave the guilt of my sin.' Have mercy on me, o God, according to your unfailing love. Wash away all my iniquity and cleanse me from my sin. Cleanse me with hyssop, and I will be clean; wash me and I will be whiter than snow. Let me hear joy and gladness; let the bones you have crushed rejoice. Create in me a pure heart, o God, and renew a steadfast spirit in me. Do not cast me from your presence or take your Holy Spirit from me. Then I will teach transgressors your ways, and sinners will turn back to you. The sacrifices of God are a broken spirit; a broken and contrite heart, o God, you will not despise."

Maria was sincerely grateful to God that His protective forces cleared her mind and heart. It was obviously a wrong time, wrong place, and wrong person for strong feelings. The Lord did not allow Maria to betray her Alex, though she was so close to it. She would tell her loved one the story of her weakness and God's disapproval of another choice.

Glory to Thee, O Lord! Glory to Thee!

Chapter 8

Since "repentant Sunday," Maria had been in a different life. There was no more excitement and disappointment. She got up easier in the morning and had more strength for the whole day. She felt herself in the process of healing from severe illness. Maria sincerely praised the Divinity in her daily prayers. She thanked for a miracle of disillusion and for saving her life again.

On Tuesday, Maria was preparing the operating room for the surgeries of the day and had a chance to think about everything that had happened to her. She always tried to analyze and understand the reasons of her deeds, particular her weakness in the case with Russian pilot. Maria was not looking for excuses, but she wanted to avoid any similar situation in the future. She felt regret that she had not recognized the delusion at once, and she was ashamed for her inability to fight the obsessive dreams, thoughts, and feelings without support of the Divinity. Presently, she blamed herself for creating the problem that might cost her a lot.

Maria could not wait until the next Sunday and her new visit to church. She needed the complete cleansing through Confession and Holy Communion. What was her disappointment, when she saw Alexander in the company of three other officers, getting into the hospital bus and taking their Sunday trip to town! She did not want to be with him in the church again. The last time she was attracted to him so much that she was not able to follow the service. She was dying for him in the fire of passion. She saw nothing around her, but his magnetic eyes, and she could hardly remove her eyes from him.

The driver, an elderly man, knew Maria well and called her name. He invited her and another woman to go to the town by the hospital bus. The driver explained that his passengers were not going to the church, but to the same town, and he could make a stop for the women where they needed. Maria exhaled with relief.

On the bus, the officers tried to talk to Maria, asking questions about her personal life. Maria avoided the detailed answers in accordance with hospital regulations. Alexander watched her with his big and sad eyes. Maybe it was just Maria's female imagination that he was disappointed about the relationship that had never existed in real life. The Divinity cancelled it at the very first signs of its development.

They arrived quickly. The church was opened, but it was early and there were only a few people inside. Maria did not experience the demonic fire and obsession in which she was burning last time. She felt ashamed that last Sunday she was not able to follow the service and did not remember a word from the priest's preaching. Maria asked God to forgive her. She asked in a way that she used to ask her own father in childhood. On that day, she enjoyed the service, Confession and her Holy Communion.

Maria thought,

"I am still afraid to meet Alexander Stern one-on-one in order not to destroy the wall of protection. What does it mean? I am still under the spell of delusion, isn't I?"

God's final settlement of the situation was not easy, and Maria lived under shock for a long time. The chief-of-staff brought the order for the relocation of the Linden Hospital further from the eastern borders of the country. Everyone from the hospital received the personal task of packing which had to be accomplished in three days.

Maria spent all her working hours between the operating room and packing huge boxes with surgical materials. Her thoughts were preoccupied with her job. She needed to label the contents of each box carefully. When Maria was back at her room at night, she had no strength for long praying, and young woman prayed shortly in front of the icon,

"O Angel of Christ, my holy guardian and protector of my soul and body, forgive me all wherein I have sinned this day, and deliver me from all opposing evil of mine enemy, lest I anger my God by my sin. Pray for me, a sinful and unworthy servant, that thou may show me forth worthy of the kindness and mercy of the All-holy Trinity, and of the Mother of my Lord Jesus Christ, and of all the saints. Amen."

In a minute or two, she was asleep.

Three days flew by and Maria did not have a chance to see Alexander Stern. On the fourth day, Dr. Kraus sent Maria to have her lunch in the cafeteria. What a surprise! The table, where the Russian officers used to sit, was empty. She noticed two more empty tables on the other side of the room.

No one had the right to ask questions about any of the patients or personnel. Maria always waited until later when the information used to be clarified by itself. On her way to the nursing station, she paid attention to the fact that the door of Alexander's room was widely opened and nobody was there.

When Maria had finished her work and came to her room, she noticed that her roommate's bed and the part of the wardrobe were empty as well. She understood: "They have already moved to a new location."

What a pleasure to stay alone in the room and pray aloud without anybody listening, interfering, or watching! Maria prayed in a calm voice, pronouncing every word of a prayer distinctly, as she was taught during childhood. After all her evening prayers she asked,

"O Lord, bless me for my night rest and make me strong for the trip to a new destination."

She thought for a while and added, "I understand that I cannot be in touch with Alexander Stern, but let me watch him from a distance and know that he is getting well."

Maria took a shower and went to bed. She picked up a strange and unpleasant feeling. In some way, the feeling was connected to the Russian pilot. There was no more of that uncontrollable strong desire to see, hear, or touch Alexander Stern. That desire made Maria crazy, ready for anything in order to meet him, stay near him and breathe the same air with him. However, a new feeling carried some threat and caused Maria's concern about Alexander Stern. Maria looked at the clock. It was midnight and she found explanation for the new shift of her senses,

"I must be exhausted."

Maria closed her eyes and a wave of white light and pleasantly gentle warmth slowly filled her and covered her body.

"Thank you, O Lord, for your Glorious protection and Divine forgiveness. Now You cleanse me with your light and rejuvenate my strength with your healing warmth. What a blessing to sense how Your light and warmth fill every cell of my sinful body! *Glory to Thee, O God! Glory to Thee!*"

The war events at the end of 1943 were unpredictable for the population of Germany and Western Europe. The Red army liberated the majority of the Soviet lands that were occupied by the Nazis. In January 1944, the Soviets advanced into Poland. Allies started bombing biggest industrial cities in Germany. The bombing by the Allies caused heavy civilian losses among the population and thousands of wounded people.

The building of the new hospital was two times larger in comparison to the Linden Hospital, but it was impossible to admit all the wounded pilots that were transported every day. The wounds and burns required longer terms for healing and the hospital rooms were overcrowded: twenty to thirty patients stayed in each room.

The chief-of-staff called the local hospitals, asking for help. As Maria learned, the situation was pretty much the same in all the local hospitals due to persistent bombing and hundreds of wounded civilian people. The hospitals were small, and they refused to keep the patients from the military hospital on their premises. The work shift for inmates was extended to 16 hours with three breaks - twenty minutes each.

Two inmates couldn't physically tolerate the tense schedule, and hospital administration sent them back to their camps. Everyone knew what it meant. One-time Maria was about to faint in the operating room during the night surgery. It was one more emergency case, and the surgery was scheduled after her day shift. Night surgeries were dangerous for Maria. She was absolutely drained of her strength by night and could faint easily.

When the hospital moved to a new location near Hannover, Maria did not meet Alexander Stern there. Maria's roommate was not at the hospital as well. She had never heard of anything about them. During the first week at the new place, her memory returned her from time-to-time to that room, where Alexander Stern got stuck between life and death during her night shift, or to the church, when the two of them were together.

In the middle of the second week, she assisted Dr. Kraus at a surgery and, thank God, it was the end of their work when he started the conversation about the Russian officers. On that day, he was grumpier than usual.

"We tried our best to fix our patients, but the war has probably other plans for them. Do you remember two Russians that we were operating on?"

Maria remembered them very well, but asked the question,

"One of them had two chest surgeries, didn't he?"

"That's right! They were in a transport that left one day earlier. The Allies bombed during the daytime and destroyed both transports, so none of them survived."

Maria felt like the ground was moving under her feet. Dr. Kraus was finishing the surgery, putting in the last stitches when the sirens announced a new bombing. He was angry.

"They are so obnoxious! They bomb days and nights. Go to the bomb shelter, Marichen. Run!"

Maria took off her gloves and moved slowly to the entrance. She did not feel like she was ready to run. Thank God, no one paid attention to her due to the bombing and chaos. Maria got into the shelter, found a spot in the corner, and started to cry. She knew it was war or probably God's way to settle a dangerous situation, but it was very painful. No doubt, the Lord had saved her life for the fifth time, but took Alexander Stern's forever. Maria whispered, *"Remember, O Lord, the soul of Thy departed servant Alexander Stern and forgive him all transgressions, voluntary and involuntary, granting him the kingdom, a portion of Thine eternal good things, and the delight of Thine endless and blessed life. Amen."*

The war fronts moved fast from the east and west. Every day there was English, American, and Russian bombing and every day there were enormous admissions of pilots to the hospital. There were hours of work without central electricity and the hospital generator could hardly supply the hospital with power. Sometimes the threat to the lives of patients forced the experienced surgeons to operate with lanterns because the repair of the central lines took too long, from ten hours to up to several days. The wounded patients were in dangerous condition and required immediate assistance.

The number of deaths increased significantly. The hospital had a shortage of medications and dressing material. The only thing in which they did not experience a shortage of was blood for transfusions. Concentration camp inmates were used regularly for draining blood. There was only one complication with donor blood – difficulties with it's delivery due to frequent bombing and ruined roads.

At the new hospital most of the time, Maria assisted the chief surgeon Dr. Kraus. He insisted in assigning her to the operating room six days a week. One day Dr. Kraus noticed that Maria was shaking at the end of a surgery. He was aware of the extended shifts of inmates and poor quantity of food that they received. The chief-of-staff mentioned at the meeting that there were days when the inmates were given one meal for two people: some soup for women and the main course for men.

Nobody considered surgeon Kraus an easy person to work with, but Maria got used to him over time.

She sensed his every motion and handed him the instruments before his request. In many cases, she was a real help in surgical work and that was a reason as to why he did not take another doctor for assistance. When the surgery was over and they were washing their hands, he asked Maria,

"When did you eat?" She did not have her voice due to complete exhaustion and whispered, "At 5 p.m., Dr. Kraus."

He looked at his watch. It was about 2:12 a.m. That surgery was an emergency case, otherwise the patient could die by morning. Dr. Kraus asked again,

"Do you have anything to eat?"

"No, Dr. Kraus. May I go?"

Maria did not know what to expect from him, the grumpy elderly man. She heard that his son was killed in 1942, and his wife could not stand the tragedy and passed away a week later. Since then, no one wanted to assist him, because no one was *good enough*. Even the German surgeons could hardly stand his sarcastic remarks while assisting him at the surgeries. With time, he preferred the "dumb inmate." He explained it once to his colleagues,

"She doesn't speak, but she has professional intuition. I prefer it to your professional discussions."

Maria walked slowly to her room; the dizziness did not allow her to move fast. The steps to the second floor seemed to move, as an escalator. One more day was over, and she had survived.

During the war, Maria learned to live without planning anything in her life or dreaming.

"Why even try to plan anything? What's the point? I have to live one day at a time, because *tomorrow* may never come."

Maria learned to believe that there was one hope and support for her: the Divinity. Each day she finished her morning prayers with the same request,

"Dear Lord, bless me for this day. Give me my strength. Help me, save me, have mercy on me, and keep me, O God, by Thy grace. Make my whole day peaceful and sinless under the protection of my Guardian Angel. Amen."

In three months, the hospital was in the process of re-evacuation again. Nobody knew where a new location was supposed to be, but three teams of prisoners were brought from nearest concentration camps for packing and loading the trucks. This time hospital administration did not want the medical personnel to be involved in packing the hospital materials because it was obvious that the personnel had no time for additional assignment.

The hospital personnel were ordered to keep their own belongings packed and to be prepared to move at any moment. The administration waited for final instructions from the higher command. Everyone understood that the war was coming to its end. If a miracle did not happen, everything was over. The chief-of-staff sent his family somewhere from the premises.

Dr. Kraus mentioned during one of the night surgeries that he could not communicate with his daughter Eliza and her three children for the last two weeks. They lived in Eastern Prussia. At that moment, he sounded like a normal caring father who was greatly concerned about his kids.

"Can you imagine, Marie that she is absolutely alone there? Her husband is on military service in Italy and at this moment nobody knows for sure if he is alive."

"Who does your daughter live with?"

"She lived there with her in-laws in a huge family estate. Her father-in-law passed away five years ago and her mother-in-law died last month. I hope that everything is all right with my girl and grandchildren, and just the temporary technical interruption does not give us the possibility to talk."

Maria replied to him in her thoughts,

"I could not be in touch with my family and Alexander for years. How could this be compared with our separation? It means nothing."

Then she imagined the situation of a woman with three kids somewhere in the woods a hundred miles from soviet troops, whose husband was somewhere on the front and who had recently lost her brother and mother. Maria felt ashamed of her first selfish reaction.

Maria thought that Dr. Kraus had read her mind when he asked about her family. Unexpectedly she answered truthfully about her fiancé in Paris, but thank God, did not say a word about her family in the

Ukraine. Surprisingly, Dr. Kraus was enthusiastic about her fiancé in Paris:

"Where does your fiancé live in Paris?"

Maria replied.

He continued,

"My sister lives in Paris too. She has been there for twenty-four years. She moved with her husband to France right after their wedding. I'll call her and she will find him."

When Dr. Kraus found out that his sister lived in the same area as Alexander's family, he affirmed, "She must know Alexander and his family."

Dr. Kraus again sounded like a normal person, but the years of slavery had taught Maria not to trust anybody.

The order for relocation was received at night. Hospital personnel were given five minutes to be on platz near the hospital. They put Maria in the same truck as Dr. Kraus. She realized that in that truck they transported the personnel of the surgical department. The next truck was moved the kitchen personnel. She could not see the rest of the trucks because it was still dark and the beans and electric lanterns were not allowed due to night bombing.

Maria learned something very important about Germans; even during the war, they kept everything in order. Everyone had to respond to commands quickly and fulfill their tasks in the best way. Any discussions and offered opinions were not acceptable. With time, Maria noticed that the war had transformed people into robots. The war switched off their feelings and emotions. Everyone followed the demands of the war.

It was difficult to imagine anything worse or more stifling than the order for inmates from German concentration camps. Death was the only punishment for not immediately following an order or failing to comply with an order one hundred percent. Any flouting was forbidden.

On the way to the new location, Dr. Kraus made some remarks regarding the last surgery. Then he lowered his voice and changed the topic abruptly:

"By the way, I called my sister at night. The phone connection was not perfect, but she understood me and promised to help."

Maria answered in a required form:

"Thank you, Dr. Kraus."

It was difficult for Maria to understand him and she thought,

"Why is this usually grumpy and self-centered person volunteering to find Alexander? He was not nice and sincere to his colleagues but now he decided to help an inmate. Why? I wonder, why?"

She was very tired after the night surgery when he asked about her family. Maria blamed herself for losing control. She mentioned the fact that nobody was supposed to know. It was a huge piece of personal information. Maria was careful about "hiding" any personal information, and all of a sudden she gave out information about her fiancé in France with a Russian last name of Kurbatov.

"Only God can protect me again," Maria thought.

Maria sat with closed eyes, praying quietly and trying to find the warmth and light within. The last two weeks were exhausting and did not give her personal time for praying. It was very disturbing. She learned to pray while working - praying short prayers and repeating them numerous times.

One was The Prayer of the Publican: *"O God, be merciful to me a sinner."*

The second was The Beginning Prayer, her favorite: *"O Lord Jesus Christ, Son of God, for the sake of the prayers of Thy most pure Mother and all the saints, have mercy on us. Amen."*

When Maria repeated those prayers more than a hundred times daily during her work, the light and warmth came in, and she felt different: not so drained, stressed, and lonely. It seemed to Maria that the presence of the Holy Spirit supported her, pushing out her inner fears and taking away everyday danger.

Dr. Kraus noticed her quiet praying many times during the surgeries. He didn't have anything against it, as long as it did not interfere with their intensive professional work. When he could not contact his own daughter for a while, he asked Maria to pray for her and his grandchildren. She did. For three days in a row, she asked the Lord and his Virgin Mother to protect Dr. Kraus' daughter and her small children and to keep them alive.

Maria also asked God to help Dr. Kraus to find them, as soon as possible. After the deaths of his wife and son, he had only Eliza and her children. Thank God, he found them. He talked to them late at night, and right after, he sent a nurse with a note to Maria:

"Thanks for your prayers. Eliza called me five minutes ago."

Glory to Thee, o Lord! Glory to Thee!

Chapter 9

The new location of the Linden hospital was near Hamburg, in the northern part of Germany. After three hours of their journey, they arrived in an area of snow and low temperature. It looked so different in comparison with their previous locations. Maria had heard her angel's voice again:

"This is your last stop, Marie."

"What did it mean? Did it mean that there was no other place for the hospital to move? It was the northern part of the country. Where else could they relocate? What are their plans about the inmates?" Maria thought.

It was difficult to guess the answers. Maria noticed how some time ago the additional tension appeared in the faces of the inmates? Nobody wanted to be executed at the very end of the war. New inmates brought terrifying stories. The fascists annihilated the inmates in many camps in eastern Germany before the Russians came. The sense of double danger was in the air.

Hospital personnel were given three hours for unpacking the hospital materials, preparing the kitchen, patient rooms, three operating rooms, dressing, and procedure rooms. The supplies for physical therapy were not delivered and the big room was empty. In three hours, the first patients were taken for surgeries.

The day was extremely long and difficult. Maria was tired to death when she went to her room. Drinking tea did not satisfy her hunger. She prayed in a new room for the first time. Maria had two roommates. Both women were sent to the hospital recently from the camp. One of them was a nurse on the night shift. Another, by the name of Annette, stayed in bed, watching Maria kneeling and praying.

Maria knew prayers in Ukrainian, German, and French. She preferred German because it was less dangerous to pray in German. She remembered the words of Alexander's mother, a Russian woman, who prayed only in French:

"God understands every language, Marie, because He created different languages for us, people".

Maria believed in her smart explanation and found nothing wrong with praying in German.

It was around four in the morning when somebody knocked on Maria's door, calling her name. Maria put on a robe on top of her pajamas, and looked out of the room. There was a guard on duty who had delivered Dr. Kraus' order to come quickly to his office. Maria wanted to change her clothes, but the guard said,

"He wanted you to be their immediately, without wasting time for putting on a uniform. You'll be back in five minutes."

Maria had no idea where Dr. Kraus's office in the new hospital was and asked the guard,

"Where should I go?"

The person on duty took Maria to Dr. Kraus' office. Dr. Kraus was talking to someone on the phone in his usual loud manner. He handed the phone to Maria.

Her heart raced, "Who could it be?"

Maria said:

"Hello?"

"Marie, my dear Marie! Can you hear me?"

It was Alexander's voice from her dream world. She could recognize it among millions of others. Maria listened and could not believe that a new miracle had happened. The tears were pouring on her cheeks and dripping on her hands. She was not able to pronounce a word.

"Marie, mon amour, I'll be at your hospital by the end of the next week, if they allow me to cross the borders. I promise to get to you, as soon as I can."

The poor young woman did not know what borders Alexander was talking about, and who was supposed to allow or not allow her fiancé to come and meet her. Maria listened, holding her breathe. She did not know that Dr. Kraus suggested for Alexander to come to Hamburg through Belgium and the Netherlands.

Maria knew one thing: she should not die at this moment, although she was very close to it. She had to survive no matter what happened tomorrow. More than anything, she wanted to see her Alex again. Alexander realized that Maria was not able to continue the phone conversation, because the shock was too strong that it nearly knocked her out.

Alexander asked,

"Marie, I would like to talk to Dr. Kraus again. Will you hand the phone to him?"

Maria returned the phone to Dr. Kraus and sat down in a huge armchair, without asking for permission. She looked like a starved kitten that was not fed for a week. Her body was losing strength. In a couple of minutes, Maria heard the bells ringing. The bells from nowhere rang louder and louder in her ears and interfered with hearing of Dr. Kraus's conversation. Maria closed her eyes: she was dying. Dr. Kraus looked at Maria, said something to Alexander and interrupting their conversation. He called for a nurse from the emergency team.

When Maria opened her eyes, she saw two nurses in the room, injecting her with something. Dr. Kraus ordered some food and it was delivered in five minutes. Real food worked better than any injections. Maria was not so dizzy after two sandwiches and a small cup of strong coffee, but she was still very weak.

The weakness in the entire body was Maria's major concern. She was afraid because the Nazis used to send weak workers back to the concentration camps and everyone knew what was in store for them there. The concentration camp was not a sanatorium or a resort, and it was not a hospital either. The Nazis quickly got rid of the useless inmates. They sent useless bodies directly to the crematoriums.

A terrible weakness did not allow Maria to keep her eyes opened: she tried to open them, but her eyelids closed within two-three seconds. She had no strength to say anything or ask about Alexander.

Dr. Kraus explained with a new sound of apology in his voice:

"I saw your nervous shock and ordered the nurses to inject the sedative medications. Now I can see that you are, probably, too weak for the dosage, Marie."

He was right. The young inmate could not stand up and walk by herself. Dr. Kraus ordered the nurses to take Maria to her room. When they were at the door, he said,

"Tomorrow is your day off. Stay the whole day in your room, resting in bed. Do not starve tomorrow. Let your roommates bring food for you."

Maria whispered,

"Thank you, Dr. Kraus."

She was happy to receive one entire day of rest, but at the same time she wanted to be sure that one day was enough to rejuvenate after the sedation.

When the two nurses delivered Maria back to her room, her roommate, Annette, looked at them in horror. They put Maria in bed and left. It took some time for the new roommate to understand that Maria might need her help and the woman brought her some water and switched on a lamp on a small table. The light was annoying, but Maria did not have strength to open her eyes, talk, or ask to move the lamp further aside. The roommate made a conclusion that something awful had happened to Maria during the twenty minutes of her absence. Annette did not ask any questions. She had learned all the rules of the inmate's life.

Annette sat next to Maria, washing her face with a wet towel. In half an hour or so, Maria opened her eyes and was surprised to see a new roommate near her bed. The woman was crying.

"Why are you crying?" asked Maria.

Annette, startled from the unexpected sound and replied,

"I thought that you were dying. You fainted there. They brought and put you in bed."

Maria smiled and whispered,

"Thank you, Annette."

Then she added,

"Do not awake me in the morning, please. Tomorrow I was given my day off."

"All right," Annette answered.

"Please, bring my food to the room. It was Dr. Kraus's order," Maria asked in a weak voice. It was her last request and she fell asleep.

There was no more church attending on Sundays. Maria wanted to find one in the area, but in accordance with the new regulation, the inmates were not allowed to leave the premises of the hospital for relatively long term. They gave her half a day each Sunday for praying at home. Maria always felt the difference between worshiping in church and at home. Only in church, she could have her Confession, Holy Communion, as well as cleanse and refill herself with the Holy Spirit.

Every time being in church, Maria sensed cleansing of the head and body through aches here and there. It lasted from minutes to half an hour, depending on the level of *soiling*. Sometimes she experienced shortness of breath in a church and a strong wish to leave, to catch some fresh air outside. She had never left the church before the end of the service. She remembered her grandfather's explanation of the initial discomfort in the church:

"The Holy Spirit is cleansing your inner dust."

Grandfather told children:

"The evil force wants people to leave the church and to stop the process of cleansing and refilling with holiness. We must be strong and do not allow evil to win."

On her *day off*, Maria woke up at ten in the morning. She still felt a little bit dizzy after the medications. She took a shower. After her morning prayers, Maria enjoyed her feast: Dr. Kraus sent her again two sandwiches and coffee. The combination of shock and medication knocked Maria down, and after breakfast, she dozed off again for another hour. The additional rest made her more balanced and Maria worshipped with enjoyment.

Maria's memory took her back to her childhood. Every Sunday, the Kotyks attended church services. All of the people sensed that the old blue church was flowed with the Holy Spirit, and it was a pleasure for them to be there. The Kotyks confessed weekly. Count Kotyk Jr. explained to his children,

"People need to confess their sins every week. It is like cleaning the house. Everyone dislikes dirty clothing and linen, dusty rooms, and sticky floors. We do not eat from the dirty dishes. The odor in a dirty house is so bad that nobody wants to live or visit it. Normally people take good care of their things and houses. What about their souls?"

Maria was the oldest child in the family, and by the age of fifteen, she learned the importance of confession. Her siblings were younger and did not see anything sinful in their behavior or deeds. Sometimes, they tried to skip the confession.

Count Kotyk Jr. reminded them:

"Every human body is the home for God's soul. The presence of souls differ us from the rest of the earthly creatures. The Creator gave us part of Him in the form of a pure and shiny soul. Our soul cannot stand sins, another form of dirt and weight. That is why we go to confession, where we name honestly all of our sins in front of the Lord. What is so important in Confession? We should not only name all our sins in front of God, but our Father expects our sincere repentance and request for forgiveness. Why should we collect dust and dirt in our souls, the material that we will never use for good?"

Maria believed that people used to start the accumulation of their sins in their childhood because the parents do not pay serious attention to the sins of their children. The church prepared parents and children for the first confession at the age of seven. It was a very important event in Maria's life. She remembered herself crying bitterly because it was not easy to announce out loud all of her sins. They were definitely childish, but her soul marked them as sins, and Maria asked God for forgiveness. Maria remembered how her Godmother and Maman were sorry for the poor child, and promised her that the Lord, who was always merciful to good children, would forgive her sins.

Maria's memories were interrupted by Gertrude, her other roommate. She came back after her work shift. She learned from Annette about Maria's night condition, and opened the door cautiously in order not to awaken her roommate.

She noticed Maria sitting in bed and asked,

"How are you now? Do you feel any better?"

Maria replied,

"Thank you. I am much better."

It was strange that somebody asked about her condition.

"Do you need anything?" Gertrude asked.

Maria smiled,

"No, thank you."

Gertrude did not ask about the reason for Maria's condition, and Maria appreciated it very much. She hated to lie, but she could not tell the truth.

Maria sat down near the window and returned in her thoughts to the phenomenon of "a sin."

Gertrude asked,

"What are you thinking about, if it is not a secret?"

"About human sins," answered Maria.

Gertrude was surprised and asked,

"What do you think about sins?"

"Do you know, Gertrude that our sins have weight? The child's small sins have light weight. Our sins are heavy. To my mind, now I understand why some people have lost inner peace in their comfortable pre-war life."

Gertrude was surprised to hear about the topic that her young roommate was interested in. She thought,

"It's interesting, but for me it is too philosophical and not easy to understand."

After a minute of silence, Gertrude asked,

"So, why do you think people lose peace and happiness?"

Maria explained it in the way she saw the problem.

"People have the tendency to accumulate many sins and do not confess and repent of them. Even being in good health and a financially stable position, they block up their souls with heavy and sticky dirt. The buried soul cannot pick up the vibration and joy of life. That's why people lose happiness."

Maria saw multiple examples from the life of her fellow students in France. She continued.

"With time, they experience constant dissatisfaction with their relationships and the quality of life. They feel envious when they see happy people and nice relationships."

Gertrude interrupted Maria with a question that had bothered her for a long time.

"Do you think that envy is fed by other human sins?"

Maria replied,

"I had a chance to see such people in school. They thought that they were very important and their fellow students were unable to notice their extraordinary talents or beauty. It was our youth and we were easily moving, enjoying our young lives, nature, studies, and trips. We visited different exhibitions, lectures, theater performances, concerts, and movies. We were dancing with pleasure, and had long discussions while walking in the park. Their high opinion of themselves did not allow them to enjoy what we liked and to feel what we felt. Then they became envious. They were envious. One sin developed the next one."

Maria looked at her roommate and asked,

"Why were we so different, Gertrude?"

Gertrude shrugged her shoulders. Maria explained,

"The answer is easy. We did not experience any extra weight that pulled us down. It did not happen due to our inborn righteousness, but because we unloaded our sins every Sunday and tried not to repeat them. Some people preferred to pull full basket of their sins for a long time, and it exhausted their thoughts, feelings, and physical body. Sometimes they pulled that dirt to the end of their lives, losing happiness, health, and hope. What can they gain instead?"

Gertrude understood what Maria meant.

"I feel sorry for them,"

Gertrude responded.

"Usually they do not unload it. On the contrary, they add to it. My sister forgot church and confession a long time ago. She knows that her life is sinful and she does not want to confess her sins. Actually, she has one repetitive sin. She understands that if she confesses and repents sincerely, she cannot do it again. Otherwise, why confess? She got seriously sick last year. I love my sister and pray for her every day."

Maria nodded in agreement, going on to say,

"Unfortunately the weight of sins can completely drain people. They do not want to admit that the real cause of their problems is their stubborn refusal to open all of their sins in front of the Lord. They cannot find strength to do it due to their weak connection with the Divinity."

Maria smiled with her special pure smile and continued,

"I was lucky that I learned during childhood that with God's blessing, we can achieve anything we want, but only with God's blessing."

Gertrude sat down closer to her young roommate.

"Do you know, Maria, some people are afraid to name their sins in front of the priest? They see a man and they cannot do it in front of him. What else I noticed? Some adults consider that they are inerrable and sinless. I have my suspicion that the evil forces are involved in these cases."

Maria told Gertrude a regrettable story about the *sinless* professor-assistant at her medical school.

Maria began her story,

"Madam Osborne received a wonderful education, got married to a nice person, gave birth to a beautiful daughter, lived in a magnificent house, and was depressed for many years. With time, her condition deteriorated. It was at the time of my graduation, when she complained to me, 'Maria, I feel a large weight on my chest. It causes discomfort and pain. It makes me tired and irritable. I checked with two professors and they did not find any pathology. Nevertheless, I feel it there. It interferes with my breathing when I lay down. What do you think it can be? I am scared.'"

Maria drank some water and continued,

"I felt sorry for Madam Osborne, and instinctively asked her about the date of her last confession. I saw that my question sounded strange to ask a depressed woman, and Madam Osborne asked me with irritability in her voice, 'What does confession have in common with my illness?'"

Madam Osborne laughed at me and said that she had never confessed because she did not consider herself such a sinner. I felt bad for her. It was obvious that she had lost the connection with the Divinity, or maybe had practiced it. The demonic forces won in her case. The woman committed suicide three months after our conversation."

Gertrude sighed and looked at the clock. It was lunchtime. She promised to bring Maria's lunch and left for the cafeteria. Maria felt tired and dizzy again, and went back to bed. She closed her eyes and dozed off. It was not a deep sleep, but a light sleep where she saw a dream. In that dream, Maria was a five-year-old child. She played with her Grandpapa not far from the church. She saw him watching her dancing and spinning. They had always enjoyed being together. He picked up Maria and spun her around. It was such a pleasure for Maria to be with her tall and strong grandpa. The child asked,

"Spin me more, please, a tiny bit more."

She laughed and flied above the green grass and bright yellow flowers.

Then she heard the ringing of the church bells, stopped dancing, and ran to the church. Maria learned from her parents that their ancestors built the blue church centuries ago. It was one of the most beautiful churches in their area, a sky-blue wooden structure with golden domes and white hand-curved plate bands around the windows. The walls were built of pine trees without a single nail. The huge lime trees surrounded the churchyard. It seemed to Maria that at that very moment she picked up the sweet smell of lime flowers.

Maria, being a small girl, started dancing on the porch of the church. Her grandpa stopped her firmly,

"Marie, we are in the house of the Lord. You cannot play or dance here. God is watching us. You must not upset Him with silly behavior."

Maria felt how the light and warmth filled her body. Maria thought,

"Thank you, Lord, for my day off and for a wonderful dream."

Glory to Thee, o Lord! Glory to Thee!

Chapter 10

On Sunday after morning worship, Maria left with Dr. Kraus' permission to the nearest library to read some poems. The town library was across the road from the Linden hospital. In case the hospital needed Maria, they knew where to find her. She was there last Sunday and had the pleasure to discuss Schiller's poetry. Frau Franciscka Muller was a wonderful librarian. Her reciting of poems was so professional. What was Maria's disappointment when this time she saw a man instead of Frau Muller at the librarian's desk! He watched Maria suspiciously, carefully examining her with his cold eyes.

Maria approached and greeted him,

"Good morning."

He answered with a question,

"What do you want to read today?"

Maria named a book that she was reading last time and had not finished. The librarian asked, without emotion,

"I need to see your ID."

Maria handed him her hospital ID. He checked Maria's identification document and went to find the book.

While waiting, Maria took a magazine from the shelf. The voice behind her asked,

"Do you like to read?"

Maria answered without hesitation,

"Very much."

It was true. Even the war and long work shifts did not reduce her inner joy while she was reading. Reading a good book took Maria back to her old peaceful life, when there was no war, danger, fear, and death. In that life, she could read, dream, and love. At least for a moment while reading, she was not a part of that ugly, inhumane, cruel, and bloody mechanism.

"My Lord, the voice..." Maria thought. "The voice is so familiar, but I cannot believe that he is here."

The shock made Maria freeze for a minute. She closed her eyes and was not able to turn around and look at him. She picked up the pleasant smell of his cologne. No doubt, her Alexander was behind her. Maria turned slowly around and looked at him. She was ready to scream, to jump, to hug and kiss this handsome gentleman, but she caught the cold look of the librarian who came back with her book and cancelled the explosion of emotions in a second.

As in a slow-moving cinema, Maria took a book and went to the reading room. Alexander wanted to follow her, but the librarian asked him to present his ID. Alexander handed over his passport. The librarian examined it and let him go. Maria was more than sure that he was calling the police right at the moment. They took their seats at the table in a nearly empty reading room. She looked at her Alexander with love and anxiety,

"O, My Lord! Why did you come, Alex? Why did you take a risk to arrive here?"

Alexander answered with his bewitching smile,

"To take you home, mon amour. You traveled too long, and I decided to interrupt your journey."

Maria could not bring her nervousness under control:

"Alex, they can come in a minute and throw me again to the concentration camp and you are in danger now. Run away, Alex! Run! I do not want you to go through any trouble. I love you so much."

Maria burst into tears. All the stored pain of her heart and soul elevated at the same moment, making the chest pain enormous. It did not allow her to inhale. Alexander took Maria in his arms and tried to calm her down.

She could not recollect anything that happened later until the moment when Dr. Kraus appeared at the police department. Her boss was furious. Maria remembered seeing him once before when he was very angry at the hospital, and then she was frightened to death. Their arrest made Dr. Kraus more furious than the previous time. Dr. Kraus thought that Maria fainted because of the police and their arrest. He jumped up to the chief of police and roared,

"How dare you arrest these people? You have nothing else to do, officers. You are doing it for fun, aren't you? You want to be sent to the front and to try on your own bones what the war means. I'll help you arrange that!"

Dr. Kraus introduced Alexander as his guest from France and a neighbor of his sister. It was truth, because in reality, they were neighbors. Two blocks separated their houses. The disturbed doctor shouted,

"How dare you arrest my guest and my personal surgical assistant? Hundreds of Luftwaffe pilots were returned to life due to her devoted work. Where were you when we were working next to the front lines under the bombs and artillery fire?"

The chief of police was not given a chance to clarify the situation. Dr. Kraus attacked him without interruption. He hit the arm-chair with his huge fist and shouted in the face of the policeman,

"You sat in your cozy armchair, in this quiet tiny town as the chief of police and did not face any life threat."

The policeman realized that the mad surgeon could be dangerous and said in his defense,

"We received a false signal from the librarian. It was he, who aggravated the whole situation. There were other people in the library, and we invited your friend and the assistant to the police station just to clarify the situation."

Dr. Kraus jumped up again and said,

"I am happy that it has been clarified and I can take both of them with me."

All three of them were in Dr. Kraus' car when several planes appeared in the sky right above the small town, dropping bombs on the houses. They were on the hospital grounds when one of the bombs exploded a short distance from the car. It turned the car on its right side. Dr. Kraus, Maria, and Alexander crawled out and ran to the bomb shelter under the hospital. The hospital was on fire. Dr. Kraus turned around, looked at Maria and Alexander and all of a sudden, suggested them to disappear.

Maria stopped and asked,

"What do you mean, Dr. Kraus?"

He looked at Maria, as her father used to look at her when he was tired and stressed, saying,

"Marichen, you need to disappear! This morning we received an order to execute all the inmates. Take my car and leave! Thank you for your prayers for my daughter and grandchildren. I'll find you in Paris. Leave now!"

Dr. Kraus handed Alexander the key. Alexander took them and said,

"Thank you, Dr. Kraus. I do not have a brother in this life, but I feel I found him now. We'll be more than happy to meet and assist you in Paris. Let us know when you arrive."

Maria was stunned. Alex took Maria's hand and pulled her out of the shelter. There was chaos all around. They tried to put the car upright, but it was heavy for two of them. They saw Dr. Kraus running toward them. The three of them were successful in righting the car. Dr. Kraus tried to shout above the noise of the bomb explosions,

"Go quickly. I will see you in Paris. Tell my older sister that I love her. Go!"

Alexander started the engine. In a minute, they were out of the gate. The young couple did not know where to go and what to expect. They had one mutual desire: to be as far as possible from that hell, fire, and death.

Maria prayed repeatedly,

"Dear Lord, be merciful and save us. Show us the road to life and happiness. Amen."

Alexander was driving for an hour in an unknown direction; they wanted to be farther away from the hospital, bombing and fire. When they read the sign with the name of the next town Alexander stopped the car. He started to look for a map in a glove compartment. He did not find any.

Maria asked Alexander,

"Where do you want us to go?"

He kissed her and answered,

"To France, mon amour, to Paris."

Maria asked him again,

"How far is it from here?"

"It's pretty far, darling. Marie, all the roads are completely destroyed. I am not sure that we can drive there. We need to take a train. It is too dangerous on the roads nowadays."

Maria was frightened, asking Alexander,

"In all the trains they check the passports in all the trains, don't they?"

Alexander replied,

"In the chaos of the bombing and fire, you could easily lose a passport with your suitcases. Now they believe it. My passport and Church Certificate that verifies our Betrothal are quite enough for the two of us."

Alexander did not know another railway station except Bremen, the one where he arrived, but he did not know if they were moving in the right direction. Another thought disturbed him. He was not sure if Bremen was still functioning after the massive bombing. Alexander then recalled that when he took a taxi to the town, the taxi driver mentioned that Bremen was the only station in the area that was still functioning. Alexander did not want Maria to be nervous. He told her with his incredibly charming smile,

"The taxi driver who drove me from Bremen was a very polite man, and every time asked me to forgive him when there was no possibility to drive around a deep indentation in the road, made by bombing. Please, Mon amour, do not ask me to apologize all the time because our road is bumpy."

It was difficult to figure out what road the taxi driver chose from Bremen. The young people decided to drive to the nearest town in order to determine their location and get the information about the nearest railway station where they could catch a train to Stuttgart.

They stopped at a pharmacy. Alexander asked Maria to stay in the car, believing that her haircut and uniform should not catch the interest of anyone. He opened the door of the pharmacy, and did not see any customers there. Alexander rang the bell on the counter. A pharmacist appeared in front of him unexpectedly fast. Alexander asked her about the nearest railway station. The pharmacist did not hide her astonishment. She looked at Alexander and asked,

"Where do you need to go?"

Alexander answered,

"To Stuttgart."

The answer made the pharmacist was even more surprised. She asked Alexander,

"Who could travel through the whole country at the present time? The bombing is everywhere. I understand that it must be necessary. "As far as I know, our railway station in Schwerin is not in service any more. It was completely destroyed the day before yesterday with night bombing."

Alexander asked again,

"Do you know any other station in the area? I need to get there as soon as possible."

The woman looked at him with sympathy and asked,

"Family matters, right? It is better for you to drive for a couple of hours south and get to the area with bigger cities like Hannover or Magdeburg. There are train stations there. I hope they were not destroyed. I haven't heard about the bombing of those cities. What I know is they bombed Leipzig for two straight nights on February 19 and February 20, and on February 22, they bombed Frankfurt. There were heavy civilian losses. I have heard that the Russian troops are somewhere in eastern Prussia. Be careful while traveling. It's not the best time for it. I'll give you a map. You should know where you are going and where the gasoline stations are. The map is old. It's a pre-war map. But it will help you, I am sure."

Alexander was grateful for her assistance. He thought,

"She heard my accent and was still very helpful."

The pharmacist wanted to add something else but stopped. Alexander thanked her and left.

When Alexander got into the car, he laughed,

"My darling, we drove in the opposite direction. Instead of Bremen, we went to Schwerin. How do you like that? The station in Schwerin was destroyed two nights ago. The pharmacist suggested to drive to Hannover or Magdeburg. The pharmacist hadn't heard anything about bombing those stations."

Maria was exhausted and hungry. The stressful news made her dizzy and nauseous. Alexander did not notice changes in Maria's demeanor. He opened the map and showed Maria the itinerary. Alexander was excited and made the decision.

"Marie, now we shall go to Potsdam and stop there for a night. Tomorrow morning we can reach the Magdeburg railway station and then go on to Stuttgart. We need the car there again to get to France, but that's later, darling. Don't worry. With the condition of these roads, our journey could take quite a long time to get to Paris. We can look at it as an adventure."

He looked at Maria and saw that all his plans were canceled in a second.

"Marie, what's wrong with you? Tell me, darling, what's wrong?"

Maria could hardly focus her thoughts to answer, but managed to say,

"I don't feel well, Alex," and then she fainted.

Alex ran back to the pharmacy. He asked for smelling salts for Maria and took four packs of cookies and water back to the car. He was relieved not to meet the first pharmacist again. All Germans were suspicious about foreigners, and could call the police for a passport check.

"I need to exchange Marie's uniform for civilian clothing,"

Alexander decided.

Alex got back into the car and put the smelling salts under Maria's nose. She opened her eyes and tried to smile, but instead she burst into tears.

"I don't want to die, Alex. I was waiting for you for such a long time. I went through so much, and it's unfair for me to die when you are with me again."

Alexander covered her face with kisses and repeated the same words.

"You are not dying, Mon amour. You are not dying."

He opened the pack of cookies.

"Look, what I have for you. You are hungry and it was my fault to start our trip without feeding you."

Maria had forgotten the smell of real food. It made her dizzy again, but she enjoyed it so much because for her it was a smell of freedom.

"Thank you, darling. You remembered my weakness. I always liked cookies and milk."

Alexander passed her a bottle of water.

"Marie, imagine that you are drinking milk."

They both laughed.

Maria moved to the rear seat and fell asleep as Alexander continued driving. In three hours, the road brought them to a small town where Alexander filled the tank with gasoline. He was afraid that the closer they got to Berlin and Potsdam, the more difficult time he would have finding gasoline. Alexander noticed that as they were approaching Berlin, the military patrol began the check-up of the documents.

They stopped Alexander at one of the control posts and the young soldier asked for the documents for check-up. At that moment when Alexander handed him his passport, a senior officer called for the soldier. The patrol soldier returned the passport to Alexander and let them go. The patrol did not see Maria in the rear seat.

Alexander thanked God, woke up Maria and said to her,

"We have to stop for a night at the local hotel, darling. They provide evening and night control. We shouldn't take a risk."

Lord, have mercy!

Chapter 11

Alexander stopped at the parking lot of a small hotel. Maria asked,

"Is it necessary for us to register and stay at the hotel? Are you sure that we do the right thing?"

"Marie, we have to stop for some rest. Tomorrow we shall continue our journey. Please stay in the car, darling. I'll check in and help you get into the room."

Maria was afraid to sleep in the hotel room without documents, but Alexander was completely calm. In ten minutes, he came back to the car and took Maria to their room. The hotel clerk did not even pay attention to Maria. Once they got to their room, they took turns showering. The exciting events of the day and inner tension made them extremely tired.

Alexander slept soundly. When Maria came out of the bathroom, she kissed him gently, so as not to wake him up. She watched him for some time. Alexander was very handsome. She admitted to herself that he had become even more handsome since 1940. Maria turned off the light and went to the window to pray,

"O Lord our God, as Thou art good and the lover of mankind, forgive me wherein I have sinned today in word, deed, and thought. Grant us peaceful and undisturbed sleep. Send Thy guardian angel to protect and keep us from the evil... Amen."

At 5:00 a.m., they were again on the road. Alexander was right: the guards at the checkpoints verified the documents only at night. He planned to pass Berlin during the day.

"We have to avoid any danger and complications," Alexander explained.

At noon, they stopped at a small plaza for lunch. A tiny restaurant was located near a consignment store.

Alexander was excited,

"Mon cher Marie, I can see a consignment store over there. We have to change your uniform for a regular civil dress. Then only people will stop paying attention at you. Let us go and find something."

For several years, Maria did not go for shopping. In her pre-war life, it was one of her weak points and she enjoyed it very much. She asked the Lord to forgive this type of overindulgence, but continued enjoying shopping at magnificent Parisian stores.

"Alex, where do you suggest to keep my clothing? Do you have any spare room in your suitcase?" Maria asked.

"Sorry, Marie, but I don't have extra room for your cloths. First of all, you put some cloths on you right there, at the store," Alexander answered with a smile. "Then we'll decide what to do with the rest."

"How do you know that we can find anything that fits me?" Maria asked.

He looked at his bride with admiration and continued,

"You are so beautiful, Marie. It's easy to find everything necessary for such a perfect woman."

Maria's paleness subsided. She was pleased with his complement. The young woman knew that she looks enormously skinny, pale and exhausted, but it was a pleasure to know that Alexander loved her the way she looked. Maria smiled and whispered, while entering the store,

"Thank you, darling."

The first thing which they bought there was a middle size suitcase. Maria packed in it her newly purchased clothing: two elegant dresses, a skirt, three blouses, some underwear, stockings, a gray knitted jacket, a hat, a purse, and two pairs of shoes. Maria was lucky that the weather was still warm and she did not need warm clothing. Alexander found a warm cashmere throw that Maria could use white travelling in the car when she sleeps in her rear seat.

When the young couple entered the restaurant for lunch, Maria looked like another person in her elegant cashmere dress. The color of the dress was royal blue. A black purse toned perfectly well with a new pair of shoes. Maria chose them because they had low heal, comfortable for walking. The black hat with thin royal blue ribbon made the most significant change in Maria's appearance. It hid Maria's exceedingly short haircut of the inmate. If presently somebody paid attention at the young people, it was due to only reason – they were a nice-looking couple.

The waiter led them to the table near the window and handed the menus. Alexander made the order. They were waiting for food and Maria asked Alexander a question that came to her mind several times,

"How come that your suitcase was in Dr. Kraus' car?"

Alexander explained the whole situation.

"Dr. Kraus gave me all the instructions. I arrived, posing as his friend, for the funeral of his brother,"

Alex smiled.

Maria was surprised.

"What is funny in this story?"

she asked.

"The funniest thing was that Dr. Kraus had never had a brother. He has only a sister and she, thank God, is in good health."

Maria asked again,

"Still, why did you leave the suitcase in his car?"

Alexander continued,

"When I arrived, I found him in the hospital and he suggested to leave the suitcase in the trunk of his car, and then sent me to the library to meet you there."

Maria liked the smart plan of her surgeon.

"Alex, I cannot understand why he decided to help me. He is not such a nice person. You watched him in the police station."

Alexander looked at Maria,

"Who could be bad to my angel, tell me? He said that you were like an angel for him. He mentioned that during our first phone conversation. He was afraid to lose his angel. In your case, a man tried to save an angel. Dr. Kraus believed that many people got to the concentration camps just because they were foreigners, lost in the chaos of the war."

Maria sighed,

"I feel sorry for him. His son was killed in Russia. His wife could not stand the son's death and passed away in a couple of days after the terrible news. His daughter with three small children is in Konigsberg, which is presently under the control of Russian troops. I am more than sure that Dr. Kraus and his children did not gain anything from this war, except the losses in his family."

"What did he do before the war?" Alexander asked.

"He was the chief-of-staff in one of the Berliner trauma hospitals," Maria answered.

"Is he a good specialist? I mean, is he a high-skilled surgeon?"

"Yes, he is. To tell you the truth, I haven't met any other surgeon in the hospital with his level of skills."

Alexander paid for their lunch and they got into the car. They continued their conversation in the car,

"My dear Marie, it is war. It is difficult to be a winner in any war, but even a winner does not gain a lot, because he pays extremely high costs for military expenses, physical strength and human losses. Those officers and soldiers who were killed, would never come back to their parents, wives and children and this is the major Universal loss."

Maria looked at Alexander and all of a sudden decided to warn him:

"Alex, I have changed a lot over these years. I was not familiar with hatred. Now I know that I hate any war. The Nazis brought death to different countries, including Germany. They lost their military people on the territories of their enemies. Now they pay for their barbarian invasions into the lives of other countries with thousands of German civilians. They sanctioned hatred, death and curse. For all these facts fascism would never be forgiven. We all paid the highest price because in a way we allowed the satanic structure to develop, grow, and gain its destructive strength."

Alexander watched Maria with interest and respect. He had not seen her earlier so pathetic and firm, talking about any subject. She used to be far from political discussions.

"You are right, Marie. All of us were too loyal to fascism. All the countries wanted to be "politically correct." Now it is obvious that we cannot agree with fascist ideas of superiority of one nation or race."

Maria continued.

"In the conquered countries, the fascists annihilated great numbers of victims. I saw their cruelty toward Jews with my own eyes, Alex."

Maria burst into tears.

"All these years I tried not to recollect what I had seen in September of 1941, but the horrible memories can disappear with my life only."

Alexander realized that the subject caused anxiety for Maria. She did not have air to breathe. He tried to interrupt her.

"Marie, my angel, mon amour, I beg you to calm down. Let us inhale and exhale together."

She sobbed loudly.

"Now the German civilian population pays for Hitler's satanic adventure with their lives and the lives of their innocent children. I am sorry for them. I hate war. O, Lord, forgive me my hatred."

Alexander knew that the brutal war was not over. He did not like the news about the Russian invasion into the territories of other countries. In order to change the subject, he mentioned that to Maria. She stopped crying and asked,

"Where are the Russians now?"

Alexander repeated what he heard.

"I've heard that they entered Poland, Lithuania, and Romania. They declared war on Bulgaria."

Maria had strong beliefs about the events.

"Alex, I am sure that the Russians offered not only the defeat of fascism, but expansion of their communism in Europe under the red banner of dictatorship of workers and peasants."

"I don't think so, dear."

However, Maria was certain.

"Alex, I was a witness to their liberation of Western Ukraine. They came to our Western Ukraine before the Nazis with their idea of equality for all the people. To make all of us equal, they expropriated, or so called "nationalized" all of the private plants, factories, banks, lands, money, jewelry, and houses of the people. They closed the churches, but opened prisons. They sent those who were against their intrusion to Siberian camps. We were lucky not to be evicted from our mansion."

Alexander doubted what Maria was telling him.

"What are you trying to say, Marie that they are ready to expropriate everything that belongs to the European people?"

Maria thought for a while and replied,

"I am not sure about all of the European countries, but they will definitely occupy Germany and forcefully plant their communist democracy. The Nazis built huge number of concentration and extermination camps where the NKVD will imprison the opponents of their communist regime. They will follow the same scenario, as they act in Western Ukraine.

The history proved Maria's words. In April 1945, the American army liberated the Buchenwald concentration camp. After the liberation, the whole world learned the horrible facts of evil Nazi cruelty and insanity. However, not so many people learned the facts that right after the liberation of the Nazi inmates, the camp was administered by the Soviet Union, and it served as a special camp #2 of the NKVD. They imprisoned 28,455 Germans who were sentenced as the political enemies and opponents of the new communist regime. In 1950, the camp was passed to the government of the German Democratic Republic with 2,415 prisoners. This fact was an example of how communist regime implemented its evil power in the foundation of new "democratic" or "communist" countries.

Alexander tried to find arguments, saying something about the movement of the Allies army in western Germany.

"America, France, and England would never allow Russia to take Western Europe under their communist control."

Maria had her own opinion regarding the situation.

"They'd better move faster, Alex. I wish the Allies could liberate Germany from fascism. At least they will not bring communism here."

Alexander did not believe Maria's assumption.

"Who needs their communism in Europe? Europe has its own political structure that has existed for centuries. The Europeans would never follow the Russian red banner of workers and peasants."

Maria answered,

"The Western Ukraine also did not invite them to come with their intrusion in our historical, political, spiritual, and cultural life. We liked our flag and we enjoyed our lives. We lived in the way we inherited from our ancestors. The soviets did not make anyone happier."

The emotional conversation made Maria tired. She made herself comfortable on the rear seat and slept most of the time until the next stop. All of the roads were in terrible condition, and their trip was difficult. The road police turned them three times, ordering to take other routes due to military marches or severe road destruction. With dusk, Alexander and Maria decided to stop in a small hotel again. Traveling at night was dangerous, not only because of checkpoints where documents were verified, but also due to constant night bombing. The young couple stopped in the suburbs of Bernau.

Alexander paid for a night's stay at the hotel, and they come to rest in their cozy and crispy clean room. The owners were nice people and invited them to have supper with the other guests in the hotel dining room. They mentioned that all of the other restaurants were already closed. It was difficult to refuse because they were hungry. They were served the traditional German dinner: a glass of Bavarian beer, hot wurstchen, a slice of liverwurst on rye bread, and sautéed cabbage.

As for Maria, she had eaten anything tastier for the last three years. When the rest of the guests left, the owners invited the young couple to drink some tea and scrumptious cherry pie. Everything was delicious. Maria was grateful to God that He brought them to that small and quiet place, and arranged a wonderful evening. No one mentioned war, bombing, or death. Everyone was tired of it. Maria's dream was to find peace, at least for that night with her beloved Alexander.

Maria gave her apology and left first to do some laundry and take a shower. She went to bed and recollected her beautiful nightgowns that were prepared in advance for her marriage. At this moment, she was disturbed with the fact that she did not have her beautiful pajamas or nightgowns. Alexander quietly opened the door of the room, thinking that Maria had fallen asleep. He did some laundry and took shower.

It was completely dark in the room due to thick and heavy curtains required during the war. Maria was excited and could not fall asleep. She thanked God for His miraculous protection during the war and the instant arrival of her fiancé to Germany when all the borders were closed. She wanted to be with Alexander forever. She missed him for so long and she did not want to lose him again. Maria could not stay in bed. She got up and went closer to the window, praying,

"O Lord our God, as Thou art good and the Lover of mankind, forgive me wherein I have sinned today in word, deed, and thought. Grant me peaceful and undisturbed sleep; send Thy guardian angel to protect and keep me from all evil. For Thou art the Guardian of our souls and bodies, and unto Thee do we send up glory: to the Father, and the Son, and the Holy Spirit, now and ever, and unto the ages of ages. Amen."

Maria returned into the bed, closed her eyes but could not relax. It was warm in their room, but she was trembling, as if she stayed outside in the middle of the night. Alexander and Maria were engaged to be married. As their priest explained, the only thing they did not have yet was the final part of the church wedding. They went through the betrothal, the most important part of the ceremony. Since the moment of their betrothal, Alexander and Maria belonged to each other, just as Holy Mary and St. Joseph. Maria liked that comparison very much. She heard that Alex was out of the bathroom.

"Alex, where are you?" Maria whispered.

"Mon cher, I thought you fell asleep. I'll be with you in a minute, Marie."

Maria was shaking. He lay down in bed near her. His body was hot. He turned to Maria, hugged her, and covered her face and neck with kisses. He tried to control his passion and be very patient and gentle. It was not easy. Years of expectation and desire made him agitated. He repeated constantly,

"I love you, Marie. You are my life, my joy, my dream, and air. I love you so much! Nothing could stop me from coming here, finding you in the chaos, holding you in my arms, kissing you and taking you with me out of the hell."

His strong hands slid down along Maria's skinny body, touching her ribs and the thick scars along them. Alexander froze for a minute and then said,

"You are so thin, Marie and these scars... You need some rest and good food. I can wait until you gain your strength again. I want you more than anything, but I can wait. I have already waited for a very long time."

He wanted to separate his body from her. Maria put her arms around his neck and said,

"I need you. I want to be yours. I cannot wait until I gain weight and strength. I do not want to lose you again. I want to belong to you from this moment and to the end of my life."

Alexander whispered, kissing her,

"I am so happy. Our love won, my darling. Even the horror of war did not diminish it for a bit. On the contrary, my love became stronger. We passed our test, darling, didn't we?"

Maria did not understand him and asked,

"What did we pass, my darling?"

He was kissing her neck, inhaling the pleasant smell of her body. That smell always made him dizzy.

"We passed the test of love, Marie. Our love won the war."

Maria said,

"I think that in all the times, the real love was victorious over war."

They were blessed to become one body, one soul, and one heart. At that night, the Creator made them the happiest couple in that German town, lost in the maze of war. It was their moment, and everything looked like there was no force created in the whole world that could separate them again. It was the victory of human love and faithfulness.

Glory to Thee, o God! Glory to Thee!

Chapter 12

The next morning, Alexander and Maria did not check out of the hotel. Alexander extended their stay for two more nights and paid for board as well. The lack of rest and food, persistent fear, and long working shifts exhausted Maria to the point that the sense of freedom, happiness, and love made her completely deprived of strength. She could not walk, and she experienced a strange sensation of being drunk, as if she drank not a glass but at least a bottle of good wine. Maria was not able to go downstairs to eat, so Alexander delivered her breakfast, lunch and dinner to the room. Every time, he knocked at the door, announcing jokingly,

"Room service for a queen."

Maria's strength completely evaporated. For a rather long time she felt herself as a balloon in the sky, that flue under the forceful blowing of the stormy wind. She did her best not to fall down. At the moment when Maria had landed, she lost her might and did not have strength to fly up again.

Presently, she experienced the same condition, as when she was under the influence of sedative medications. Maria could not talk normally and she whispered. She was not able to walk without support, but she still wanted to kiss her husband and to make love with him. She wanted to prove that from now on, every fiber of her body belonged to her Alexander. The exhaustion and malnutrition were severe. She found herself falling asleep in the middle of a conversation. She wanted three things: to love Alexander, to eat, and to sleep. She smiled again in her dreams, as she used to do when she was a small girl. Alexander was sitting for hours in an armchair, admiring the beauty of his wife.

He would like to leave the country as quickly as possible and to get back to France. Only one thing was obvious: Maria was too weak to continue their journey. Being a physician, he comprehended well the danger of her weakness and concluded that they should stay at the hotel until Maria's health improved enough for her to travel. Other than that there was one more reason for extension of their stay: Alexander also liked that cozy room where Maria became his wife.

Alexander blamed himself for his impatience, "It was obvious that Maria was too weak for an intimate relationship."

He watched his wife, while she was sleeping soundly, and thought,

"Who could stand to be with my sleeping beauty in one bed after so many years of separation and not touch her?

He came up and gently kissed her lips. She answered with her smile,

"I am sorry, darling. I am so weak. I should be exhausted to death."

On the third day, the young couple came to the dining room for their dinner. Alexander asked the owners about the nearest functioning railway station where they could take a train to Paris. Frau Keener was surprised to learn that they were from France. She asked with unhidden curiosity in her voice,

"What are you doing in Germany at this dangerous time?"

Maria explained,

"I lived in Germany, but got married to my prince in France. We had graduated together from Sorbonne University right before the war. I returned to Germany and worked in the hospital. Alex worked in the hospital in Paris."

Frau Keener asked again,

"How did your husband manage to find you here?"

Maria laughed,

"It was our friend who arranged everything for us. He is also a surgeon and during the war, he worked in the same hospital with me. After the massive bombing of Hamburg and suburban towns, our hospital was completely destroyed and burned in a fire. The patients, who survived that bombing, were transported to different hospitals in the area. We became unemployed. I decided to go to France, but our friend considered this trip too dangerous for a woman to travel alone. He called my husband secretly for me and asked him to come and take me from here."

Frau Keener exclaimed,

"What a pleasant surprise! I can imagine how happy you were to see your husband in Hamburg."

Frau Keener looked at Alexander and continued,

"He was probably even happier to find his wife alive."

"You are absolutely right, Frau Keener. It was one of the most significant days in my life. I will keep it as my best memory."

It was the best explanation of the reason why two foreigners stayed in Germany at that uncertain time. Frau Keener promised to call her sister in Berlin right after dinner and to find out the nearest functioning railway station in the area.

Her husband did not take part in the conversation, but he watched the young people with interest and listened attentively to everything they asserted. Alexander got a suspicion: "For the years of the war, this man learned to be quiet. He probably did not speak a lot, but wrote many reports to the local police about their guests."

Taking into consideration the owner's "strange" behavior, Alexander did not know what to do. He supposed, "Maybe we should not wait until we get to the police unit again with the help of these nice people?"

Alexander decided not to share his suspicion with Marie, but to try finding out some information besides the owner and her sister. When Maria slept in their room after dinner, he drove to fill up with gasoline at the nearest gasoline station.

Alexander could not make a decision for the first time in his life. At the gasoline station, he found out that it was true that Russian troops were in Poland and Romania, very close to German borders. The second news was that there was no railway station in service in the nearest cities. The bombing destroyed all objects of important communications. At present time, there was no way to get to Paris by train.

It was a nice warm day at the beginning of autumn. Alexander drove slowly along the streets of the town. The town looked uninhabited. There were few pedestrians in the streets. He could feel a heavy sign in the air. The town was terrified, waiting for an unpredictable end of the war, and the arrival of Russian troops. No one could foresee anything. Alexander did not know either what to expect. He asked the Lord, *"Help us, save us, have mercy on us and keep us, O God, by Thy grace. Glory to the Father, and to the Son, and to the Holy Spirit, now and ever, and unto the ages of ages. Amen."*

When Alexander returned to the hotel, Maria was awake, impatiently waiting for her husband.

"What did you hear, darling?" she asked.

He brought her the news about the Russians. The second news about destroyed railway stations and their inability to get to Paris by train was of bigger disturbance for the Kurbatovs. Alexander and Maria did not know what to do: to leave or to stay.

"Alex, if we leave, then where should we go?"

Alex answered with another question,

"If we stay here, then for how long, mon amour?"

Alexander noticed how Maria tried to wrap herself in the throw. He did not have energy for warming her thin body. Alexander changed the topic,

"We definitely need to buy some warm clothing for you, Marie, in case we stay. In a week, it could be cold and I do not want you to get sick. You are too weak, even without additional complications."

Maria smiled. She liked his thoughtfulness. She pulled him down to the sofa and kissed him.

"I love you, Alex."

"I love you too, Marie. Well, dear, we need to decide what to do."

Alexander sat down near his wife, holding her in his arms. They were sitting for some time in silence.

"Do you know, Marie, what I am thinking?"

She turned her head toward him, waiting for his further explanation. Her face was close to his. Alexander looked at his wife and forgot about his important thought. He saw her eyes and lips, and experienced dizziness again. He covered her face with dozens of kisses, and could not separate himself from her lips. Maria pushed him gently and asked,

"What do you think?"

"What is it about?"

Alexander tried to catch his last thought and burst into laughter.

"Marie, what do you do to me? When I see your eyes, I lose my mind and forget my own name."

He concentrated at recollecting of his last thought.

"Oh, yes! I got it! I wanted to make a suggestion not to stay here but to drive to Saarbrucken or Baden. It is better to stay there for some time, closer to France. We should wait, Marie, there, until the borders are opened again. Now I see additional danger in staying in such a close distance to Berlin. Trust me, mon cher, it is too unsafe. What do you think about everything?"

Maria kissed him and answered,

"You are wonderful! I agree, it's better to go and wait there than to stay here, far away from France."

It was 5:30 in the morning, when Maria and Alexander left the hotel and continued their trip to the southern Germany, closer to their destination. Maria ended her morning prayers with the words,

"Lord, have mercy on us; for we have hope in Thee. Be not angry with us greatly, neither remember our iniquities; but look upon us now and deliver us from our enemies. Help us, save us, have mercy on us, and keep us, O God, by Thy grace. Amen."

While she prayed, Alexander was blessed with a new decision. He chose not to drive through Berlin. He believed that they conducted 24-hour patrols there, so he took the road to the west in the direction of Wolfsburg. Maria was in the back seat, and quickly fell asleep. She could not stay awake in the car for longer than half an hour due to monotonous sounds of the engine and Alexander's cautious driving. Alexander looked in the mirror and saw the pale face of his wife, her malnourished and skinny body, concluding that she required months of recovery.

"It was right that we did not stay there, waiting for Marie to feel better. That would not happen in a week," Alex said to himself.

Maria stayed with him the entire time, but he missed her voice and smile while she was asleep. His thirst for her became stronger and stronger. It seemed to him that he would never satisfy that thirst, at least in the near future. She became his magnet that completely attracted his thoughts, feelings, and body. He was unable to separate himself from Maria. He desired to see her all the time, to kiss, to love, but most of all he wanted to save Maria and make her happy.

Alexander was overwhelmed with strong emotions, responsibilities, and hardships. He started his man's talk to Lord,

"I am grateful to Thee, o Lord, for saving of my wife, my personal survival and for giving me a chance to find Marie in the fire of war. Oh, Lord, forgive me my sins and please, help me to make Maria healthy and happy. Her life was so dreadful that she could not get her strength back without Your miraculous healing. Please, help her to restore her inner peace and bring her to good health. I swear to Thee, my Lord, to be a devoted husband and always stay with her. I'll do my best in order not to lose my wife again."

Alexander looked at his wife again and thought,

"I need to feed Marie. She needs to eat every four hours. Her stomach has shrunk due to lack of food, and now she can eat only tiny portions. It's not healthy at all."

He stopped at a small café and turned to Maria. She watched him, smiling.

"Alex, I am sorry, but I am hungry again."

"That's wonderful, my queen." Alexander joked. "I read your mind and I am willing to invite you, Your Grace, to a wonderland of food."

Maria laughed: he sounded again like her Alex from the pre-war time. She felt herself the happiest in this world because the Lord returned her Alexander, a prince and defender from a fairytale life. *"Glory to Thee, o Lord! Glory to Thee!"*

After lunch, Alexander checked with his map and found the next point of destination – Gottingen. Maria sat in the car for some time and watched the beauty of multicolored fall nature. It was a pleasant sunny day in September. The traffic was moving fast. Everyone wanted to reach the destination point before dusk. The authorities forbade driving with the beans on. Alexander was happy seeing that his angel chose the right way. In comparison with many others, this road was not badly destroyed. Every night, the Allies provided the massive bombing of western Germany and at the same time, the Russians bombed the eastern part of the country.

Maria thought, "Alex's angel helped us greatly, when have moved us to the central part of the country. Glory to the Lord, the central part was less damaged."

Maria had a strong desire to talk to Alexander about her life without him, about the life threatening events since she had left Paris. She wanted him know how the Nazis took her from her family, about all the tragic events at Gulliver's farm, and her escape. She wanted to tell him about the cruel tortures in the concentration camp and, the Nazis' merciless plans to burn her, along with the inmates of the old barrack. Maria wanted to complain at the exhausting shifts at the Linden hospital that drained her physical strength and to unveil the truth about Alexander Stern.

She also wanted to learn more about his life in the country, occupied by Nazis, and about his mother. Alex had mentioned already that Countess Kurbatov missed Maria and prayed for her surviving every day during the war. However, Maria could not find strength for long conversation. Being overwhelmed with strong emotions and desires, Maria dozed off again. She bowed and touched the driver's seat with her head, and it was dangerous to drive this way. Alexander stopped the car on the curve of the road and helped her lie down in the rear seat, covering her carefully with cashmere throw. After that, they continued their journey.

Alexander drove fast, and arrived in Gottingen at 6:45 p.m., fifteen minutes prior to the road patrol. He drove along several streets, looking for the hotel for a night. Maria was awake and worried that they could not find a place for rest and supper. The road was not easy. Alexander was good at driving, but if they wanted to continue their trip the next day, he needed a good night sleep. By that time, both of them were hungry again.

Maria started to pray repetitively,

"Dear Lord, look at these travelers and help us to find a place to stay. Make that place secure and peaceful. Amen."

Within five minutes, they stopped at a magnificent two-storied hotel in the center of town. On both sides of the hotel, there were completely destroyed houses. Maria said,

"Alex, look, the Lord was merciful to this place. All the houses were ruined and the hotel looks so beautiful."

Alex parked the car and they went to the hotel. Maria stroked the marble lions on both sides of the entrance. Alex laughed at her childish gesture.

"They can bite, Marie. Be careful."

There was no doorman at the moment, and Alexander played his part of opening the heavy door for the young lady. The couple found themselves in a beautiful castle of the eighteenth century.

"What a beauty!" Maria whispered.

Alexander added,

"Thank God it was not destroyed or burned in the bombing."

A very large crystal chandelier fell down in cascades from the ceiling of the second floor. The real Persian rugs covered the well-polished wooden floors. The rugs were beautifully designed with bright palm leaves and parrots. The antique furniture from the eighteenth century and the beauty of the walls and ceiling murals transferred Maria to the castle that belonged to her mother. There she saw unforgettable wall and ceiling paintings. There was the same technique of the masters, or maybe it was painted at the same time.

Maria assumed,

"Alex, this castle is beautiful but I wish you could see my mother's castle, her inheritance from the grandparents. I am confident that the Italian artists and sculptors completed the art works in the 18th century of this castle and my mother's place. They are so much alike! They belonged to the same Italian art school.

Even if the German artists had painted in this one, they studied the art in Italy. I am more than sure about it."

The real palm trees and the bushes of blooming hibiscus surrounded a fountain in the middle of the hall. This composition made the hall of the hotel exquisitely exotic. Maria sat down in one of the armchairs and Alexander went to the register desk. He checked in, received a key, and returned to Maria.

"Dear Alex, what is this? Do I sleep and this is my amazing dream?"

Alexander liked Maria's admiring of the castle. He thought, "She hadn't seen anything beautiful during four years of horrible war and slavery. However, one thing is obvious: my Marie preserved a sense of art, beauty, and magnificence. What I always like about her is her ability to enjoy it."

"Let us go, Marie, you need to eat."

They went to their room on the second floor. The room was spacious. It looked two times larger than the rooms in previous hotels, and the paintings and furniture looked splendid. Maria noticed,

"The owners must have a designer's taste. Everything matches so well."

Someone knocked at the door. It was a maid from their hotel.

She reminded them,

"Our supper is served from seven to ten, and the dining room is downstairs in the middle of the right wing."

Maria and Alexander took shower, changed their clothes, and rushed downstairs. When the Kurbatovs entered the dining room, the owners came up and greeted them,

"Welcome to our hotel! My name is Paula Miller and this gentleman is my husband."

"I am Hermann Miller. Welcome to our place."

Frau Miller showed Maria and Alexander their table, and the waiter followed them with two menus.

Maria looked around and said,

"The dining room is too small for this place, isn't it, darling?"

"It depends on how many rooms they have, Marie."

Alexander studied the menu.

"It contains some rather interesting things, mon cher."

Maria concentrated her attention on the menu for two minutes, and her hunger made her choose quickly. They ordered and while waiting, Maria observed the guests and owners. The Millers were in their early fifties. They looked very presentable. The guests were well acquainted with the Millers and enjoyed their company in the dining room.

The waiter brought out two glasses of French wine, a complementary drink from the owners. Maria and Alexander thanked them and asked the waiter to bring a bottle of mineral water.

"Alex, I don't think that I can drink my wine. I feel that I am tipsy most of the time without it."

Alex looked at his wife with a smile and suggested,

"Don't drink it on empty stomach, mon amour. Eat first."

The waiter delivered their food. Maria looked at the liver under the onion sauce and said,

"I am sorry, but they do not have a good cook at their place. It is not prepared professionally. I wish, I can cook it."

Alexander was surprised to hear such a statement. Maria did not cook the simplest dishes when they were students. He asked,

"Marie, darling, when did you have a chance to learn professional cooking?" Maria looked at him and realized that Alexander did not know her at all. He knew nothing about her and her life from the day of their separation after her graduation from the University school.

Suddenly a weird and terrifying thought struck the young woman,

"Oh my God, he is probably in love with that girl and has nothing in common with new me. I am a stranger to him."

They ate their supper in silence and an unpleasant tension surrounded the young couple. Alexander was persistent.

"Dear Marie, tell me please, when and why have you learned a real culinary art?" Maria wanted to answer only that question.

"It was in a small town not far from Frankfurt-on-Mine."

He wanted to ask something else, but Maria interrupted him.

"One day I'll tell you, Alex, the whole story about my unbelievably difficult and dangerous life for the past four years. I survived only with God's blessing. I learned to feed and milk cows, clean the barns, bake, and cook professionally. I translate fluently from and into Ukrainian, Polish, Russian, Latin, French, German, and Czech. I can treat the patients and assist the surgeons. Now I learn something new."

"What is it, darling?"

"I learn to love you, as a wife."

Alexander looked at Maria with surprise. It was difficult for him to realize what she learned during the four years of their separation.

She was close to bursting into an anxiety attack again. Alexander noticed it and recovering from unexpected information, said,

"Marie, you are my wonder and beauty. Please, calm down. I love you more and more. God saved you for me, darling, because I could not imagine my life without you."

Maria smiled but her eyes filled with tears. She tried to pull her together.

"All these years in hell, I believed in God's mercy and your love, Alex. My faith helped me to survive."

Glory to Thee, o Lord! Glory to Thee!

Chapter 13

After supper, Maria felt tired and sleepy again. Again, she wanted to talk to Alexander about their lives during the war, but did not have any strength for it.

"Alex, I have finished my meal and have become so tired that I can hardly sit. Let us go to our room."

They thanked the owners and went upstairs.

Maria was glad that she took a shower before supper. Half a glass of good French wine relaxed her to the point that she could barely walk. Alexander helped her take off her dress. He prepared the bed, and she dove into the forgotten fluffiness of luxury down bedding.

"Dear Alex, forgive me, but I am falling asleep."

The last word was left unpronounced at the very end, as Maria fell asleep.

Alexander sat down in a deep comfortable armchair across the room, watching his wife sleep. She was smiling again like a child in her dreams. For the first time in his life, he experienced the state of bliss.

"Some time ago I could not imagine that one day after driving a very long distance across the bombed hostile country, that I would prefer sitting and admiring my sleeping wife to my own rest. Thank You, God, for showing me what means real human love."

Alexander took a map from a table and checked the itinerary for the next day. He thought,

"It would be really great if we can reach Mannheim tomorrow."

He suspected that it was too far, but the euphonic condition made his wishes determined. Alexander underlined two points on the map, Darmstadt and Mannheim, and left it on the table.

"We definitely need to avoid going through Frankfurt tomorrow. They continue bombing the industrial cities every night. It's less dangerous to make a stop in a small town, but not too far from the main road."

Alexander looked at his wife, and she smiled again. She was so sweet at this moment and did not look pale at all.

"You are wonderful, Marie. You are my Sleeping Beauty. You cannot imagine how strong my love is and how much I want you to be free and happy again."

He switched off the light and slipped into the bed. Maria turned with her back towards him. Alexander nuzzled his nose in her hair, breathing in the miraculous smell of freshness and flowers. In a couple of minutes, he fell asleep.

The night passed quickly. The next morning, the young couple checked out of the hotel, leaving at 6:45 a.m. Maria was not able to pray all of her morning prayers. She did not feel well again. Alexander helped his wife lie down in the rear seat and covered her with her warm throw. He drove through the center of the town looking for a gasoline station. It was smart to fill in the gas tank before the ride.

"My next stop for gasoline, I would arrange somewhere in the middle between Gottingen and Frankfurt. It could be Bebra," Alexander thought.

Then his thoughts returned to Maria's condition. He glanced at his wife and made a conclusion,

"In Bebra I will feed Marie. Yesterday, Marie looked so wonderful and today she is pale and weak again. Our long daily rides definitely drain her strength. Poor Marie, I wish we could move faster and reach Bebra. There I will take you to eat. O Lord, support us in our journey and bless Marie with strength."

In an hour or so, the road police stopped the traffic and turned it in the direction of Erfurt. The road to Erfurt was in poor condition, and the traffic moved slowly with frequent stops. During one of the stops, Alexander took out his map and checked how he could get to Bebra. It was impossible.

Maria woke up and asked,

"Where are we now?"

"In the middle of nowhere, my darling. I wish I knew exactly where we are, but it is difficult to determine," Alexander replied.

In a minute, all of the motion on the road was brought to a halt. Maria and Alexander looked out and saw planes coming toward the road. People were leaving their cars and running in different directions off the road. Alexander shouted quickly,

"Marie, get out of the car and run!"

She was out of the car, but could not run at all. Her terrible weakness allowed her only to walk slowly, slide down an embankment next to the road, and hide in a hole left by a bomb. Alexander was out of her sight. She heard his voice for a few moments calling her,

"Marie! Marie!"

The noise of the heavy planes came closer and closer, and Maria did not have strength to shout above the noise so that Alexander could hear her. Maria saw how three planes were simultaneously dropping bombs on the road about a mile from them. The road was packed with different cars, some of them on fire. The planes flew on. The poor travelers were left to watch the burning fires and listen to the screams of the wounded and burned people in the bombed out areas.

Maria climbed up the road and saw Alexander running in her direction. He embraced her and asked,

"Where have you been, Marie?"

She showed him with her finger,

"In a bomb-hole, near the road."

The planes were bombing objects some distance from the road. Everyone understood the danger of staying there. Maria said,

"They could bomb us again on their way back. They always do it."

The Kurbatovs noticed how the cars behind them started to move backwards. Alexander suggested to Maria to follow them.

"Mon cher, there is no way for us to drive forward. It will take some time for the road service and police to clear up the road. On the other hand, staying here is very dangerous. Let us move backward. The local people might know better how to get to another highway."

The moment they got to the other road, they saw the same three planes approaching the place where they made their previous stop. The planes bombed the cars that were still there on the road. New waves of explosions and fire covered them. Maria prayed,

"Lord, have mercy! Lord, have mercy! Lord, have mercy! O Lord, Jesus Christ, Son of God, for the sake of the prayers of Thy most pure Mother, our holy and God-bearing fathers, and all the saints, have mercy on us. Amen."

Alexander saw that Maria was trembling. The traffic on their new road was moving quickly and it looked like all of the drivers wanted to get away from the bombing zone as fast as possible.

"Marie, try to read the name of the road," Alexander asked her.

He also looked for the route number or the name of the road, but he wanted somehow to distract Maria's attention from the tragic bombing.

From a distance, Alexander saw the name of the road. Maria read it out loud. Alexander passed her the map, asking to find that road on the map. Alexander explained,

"From this point, try to find the connection with any other route that will take us in the direction of Frankfurt."

"Alex, all the roads are small, there are no connecting highways. Are we going to take the small roads to get to Frankfurt? It will take extra time!"

Maria talked to him, and stopped shaking.

Alexander noticed,

"It is better to move slower and avoid the bombing. Look, this road is small, but the traffic is rather speedy now."

Maria was hungry.

"Alex, are we going to have lunch soon?"

"We can stop at Erfurt before we go to Wurzburg."

Maria was surprised to hear a new destination point and asked,

"Why is it Wurzburg?"

Alexander explained,

"You were asleep when they turned us in another direction due to military marches."

Then he added,

"Marie, my objective is to get closer to the borders of France. I have no idea how we should get to France because all the borders are closed. But I believe that very soon the war will come to an end."

Marie looked at the map.

"I am not sure, mon cher, that with this road and the heaviness of the traffic, we will be able to get anywhere further than Meiningen by the end of the day. I can be absolutely sure of the only thing: both of us are hungry."

Maria started to pray in order to calm down, but she was out of strength after the new stress with bombing. Her prayers were interrupted frequently with the necessity to catch the breath and rest. Maria did not want to show her weakness to Alexander, but her voice sounded quieter and slower. She put aside her prayer book, because the tears in her eyes did not allow her to read. She whispered with bitterness in her tone,

"I am sick and tired of this war, of everyday danger and death. Dear Lord, help us get safely anywhere where we can stay for a while and nourish us. Our everyday rides kill my strength and I have no time for rejuvenation."

The hot tears poured down her cheeks, as she continued praying,

"Dear Lord, heal me, please. I do not want to cause any trouble for my husband. If something happened to me, it would be a disaster for Alex. You made him a devoted man. He is ready to die for me. He took a risk coming to a hostile Nazi country to find and save me. Help me, O Lord, not only for my sake. He is well-deserving of the best in his life."

Alexander could not hear Maria's prayer, but he picked up with all of his senses that she was not well.

"Marie, mon amour, what's wrong? Do you want me to stop right now?"

Maria collected all of her strength and answered in the loudest voice, she could,

"I am quite all right, Alex. I was just praying. As you know, praying always makes me emotional."

The ride on that day was the most exhausting, with a single stop before dusk. Even so, they barely reached the town of Meiningen, which Maria had mentioned after the bombing. The town was smaller than Gottingen. They found a hotel in the center of the town. The hotel was not a castle, but a regular one. Maria stayed in the car while Alexander went to check if there was an available room for them. The answer was, "None." The hotel desk clerk gave him the address of another hotel within a five-minute drive. Alexander stopped at the second hotel, when it was completely dark outside.

"Marie, will you pray, darling? We need to find a lodge and board here."

Alexander left and Maria started to pray *Our Father*. She repeated it for the fifth time, when she saw Alexander coming. He was smiling. Alexander opened the door of the car and let Maria out. He bowed theatrically, offering his hand for support.

"Your Grace, the prayer was answered, and your lodge and board are ready." Maria blessed herself with a cross and replied,

"Glory to Thee, O Lord! Glory to Thee!"

Then she smiled to her husband and said,

"And you are great, Alex. I love you so much. The world lost a great actor, mon cher."

While walking from the car, she noticed that the houses on both sides of the hotel were either seriously damaged or completely destroyed.

"Look, Alex, God preserved the hotels in both cases."

Alexander did not understand in what cases the hotels were preserved and asked to clarify,

"What do you mean, Marie?"

Maria was entering the hotel and explained,

"Do you remember the castle? Everything around of it was damaged and burned from the bombing, but the hotel was untouched. Here it is the same thing."

Two elderly people walked in front of them, speaking in French. They could not hear well and due to deteriorated hearing, they spoke loudly. Having zero desire to listen to their conversation, Maria and Alexander could easily overhear them. The elderly lady was excited about the news. She could not wait to get into the room to discuss it.

"Michel, it was one of the best dinners for the last five years, wasn't it? I enjoyed Leon's company. Did you hear what Leon said? The Allies move fast. They started from Normandy in June, liberated Cherbourg at the end of July, in August they liberated Paris and Marseilles, and in September Le Havre. Maybe we are blessed to see our Fritz and his family pretty soon. I miss them so much. Since our house was destroyed, we did not hear anything from them. The phone connection was interrupted earlier, but remember, we used to receive from them at least one letter per month. The grandchildren sent their drawings with very funny characters. Do you remember, Michel, how Lucie arranged the gallery of their drawings? Poor Lucie! The war took lives of so many people..."

The gentleman did not pronounce a word; he just shuffled with his feet and nodded in agreement to what his wife said.

Maria and Alexander were listening unwillingly to the story of somebody's family. The couple stopped in front of the door to their room. Maria did not want to confuse them and asked in German,

"In what room do we stay, darling?"

Alexander answered,

"Room 27."

The room was across the hall from the French couple's room. The gentleman looked for a key but could not find it. Alexander stopped and asked,

"Do you need any help?"

The lady answered,

"Thank you for offering your assistance. He does not hear well. I think we are all right."

The gentlemen opened the door simultaneously with the Kurbatovs. They looked at each other and smiled.

Maria got into the room and immediately fell into bed. She was extremely tired.

"Alex, allow me to not go for supper tonight. I prefer to have longer rest than to go to eat."

Alexander checked her pulse and answered,

"No, mon amour, absolutely no. We shall go and have our supper together, but first of all, we'll take a shower. After our long daily trip, that will definitely refresh us. Then both of us will go to the dining room. Be careful, Marie. I cannot stay hungry, otherwise I'll eat you. You know me."

Maria smiled. With a facial expression of a scary beast, Alex picked up Maria from the bed, spun her around the room, and brought into the bathroom. He helped her to undress, and placed her in a huge tab. She screamed when he opened the shower, because the first streams of water were rather cold.

Alexander stepped back and admired the perfectness of Maria's shape. He enjoyed watching how the streams of water ran along her beautiful young body. Washing her hair, Maria could not see the way she watched her. The smell of her soap was wonderful. It spread all over the bathroom, elevating his desire to embrace her and love again.

Alexander smiled to himself and thought,

"My Lord, I feel embarrassed and sinful, but I love Marie. Thank You for saving her. I cannot exist without my wife, without watching her, smelling her hair, touching her body, and kissing her from head to toe."

Alexander helped Maria with the faucets and continued thinking,

"I wonder, for how long is a man obsessed with his wife? Does it last forever? Sometimes, yes. As for my parents, it lasted to the end of their mutual life. I wish we can also preserve the strength of our feelings to the end of the life."

He helped wash Maria's back and feet not only because she was very tired and could not do it, but because his desire to touch her was very strong. Alexander was angry with himself and tried to force his eagerness under control.

"I am so selfish. Marie is weak, exhausted, malnourished, and underweighted. How can I even think about making love?"

After shower, he wrapped Marie from head to toe in a bath sheet and brought her into bed.

"Have some rest, mon amour, while I am in the bathroom," Alexander suggested.

He turned around and walked into the bathroom. In five minutes, he completed his shower, and stepped out of the bathroom wearing only a towel on his hips. Maria had not moved since he had left her. She smiling, seeing her husband. Alexander felt awkward that she could notice the strength of his eagerness.

"Alex, I love you. I feel sorry for my weakness."

Alexander answered,

"I love you too. I know that I have no right to touch you now and I can wait as long as you need me to wait."

Alexander sat down near her, looking in her eyes.

"Marie you have fever, your eyes are shiny."

She whispered back,

"I don't think so, mon cher."

Marie sat down in bed, put her arms around his neck, and kissed him gently.

"Oh Marie, no, please let me go. I know that today was not your best day. Not now, mon amour. We can do it tomorrow or the day after tomorrow."

She picked up his intonation.

"Or in France? Alex, I want you now. I don't want to wait for a better time. I am blessed to become your wife now."

They were again one body, one heart, and one soul. It was their celebration of surviving one more day in the terrible chaos of war.

Glory to Thee, o Lord! Glory to Thee!

Chapter 14

At supper, Maria and Alexander met the owners of the hotel. Maria was sure that the name of the hotel "Benedikta" in Meiningen was named after the owner. She was wrong. The owners introduced themselves as Frau Elsa and Herr Kurt Schulenburg. Maria mentioned her supposition about the hotel name. Frau Elsa laughed.

"It was purchased with this name fifteen years ago. We did not change anything."

The owners returned to their table and continued their meal. Maria and Alexander were hungry, and ordered a large supper with a beer for Alex and something for Maria's breakfast for the following morning.

"I realized my mistake, Marie. I was not supposed to leave in the morning without some food for you, darling. Our trips are absolutely unpredictable nowadays, and we have no idea where we can stop and eat our breakfast and lunch."

Maria watched Alexander with a smile. She did not say a word, but he answered her thought regarding some light breakfast for tomorrow. She ordered a breakfast for two.

At night, the couple was awakened by the annoying sound of sirens, as a warning of bombing. Maria had learned the sound very well and jumped out of bed quickly.

"Alex, get dressed. They have a basement. I saw the signs and arrows. Move fast and do not forget to take the documents and money. Can you hear me, darling? Take just the documents and money."

Alexander remembered that his wife was used to working in a military hospital. She was ready to go in three minutes. The explosions came closer and closer to the hotel. They rushed downstairs. The basement was under the hotel building and looked spacious. It was obvious the owners did not use their basement for anything else except a bomb shelter. The room was furnished with comfortable chairs and a couple of artificial palm and lemon trees. There were two magazine tables with piles of magazines and newspapers. The lanterns and candles were on. The electricity did not work during the bombing. Two large lanterns hung in the room, but they did not make enough light. One more lantern was on the console table near the door to the restroom. Another was inside of the restroom.

"The owners seem to be very considerate people," Maria thought.

Twelve people were sitting in the shelter. The guests of the hotel did not keep any conversation going. They were tense, listening to every sound outside. Two explosions were in close distance to the hotel.

Alexander noticed,

"Marie, I cannot see the elderly French couple. They did not come to the shelter."

Maria got nervous and mentioned it to the owners,

"We do not see our neighbors across the hall. To my mind, they have a problem with hearing. Maybe they did not hear the sound of the siren."

Alexander suggested without any hesitation,

"I can run upstairs to wake them up."

The owners looked at him with amazement.

"That is very generous," Mr. Schulenburg said.

Fortunately, the bombing was over. People went back upstairs but no one could fall sleep again.

After the bombing, Alexander went outside to check his car. The street was blocked with the ruins of two buildings across the street. Some people were walking around them. A young woman was sitting on the rubble, crying bitterly.

Alexander thought,

"We could hardly move forward today because we do not know what was destroyed in the area. Can it be that there is no way to get to the highway? Absolutely. It is better to stay in the hotel than to be trapped in the middle of nowhere. One more reason for staying here for another day: we do not know the condition of the highway after the bombing."

Alexander's thoughts were interrupted with a new sound of sirens. He saw three planes in the sky. They were only a short distance away. Alexander rushed to the hotel and met Maria on the stairs. At that time, the elderly couple was also coming to the bomb shelter. When the Kurbatovs entered the shelter Maria asked,

"Where have you been, Alex? I looked for you everywhere and worried a lot."

"I am sorry, Marie that I did not tell you. I went outside to check for our car. It was not easy to find it due to thick layer of dust that covered all the cars on the parking lot. Most of them are off white now," Alexander explained.

"Our car..." Maria repeated with a smile. You mean, you went to check for Dr. Kraus' car or maybe you had left him the document of expropriation?"

The bomb explosions from somewhere east from the hotel interrupted their conversation.

Maria began to pray,

"O Lord, be merciful to us, sinners. Let Thy mercy, O Lord, be upon us, according as we have hoped in Thee. Lord, Thou hast been our refuge in generation and generation. O continue Thy mercy unto us that know Thee. Holy God, Holy Mighty, Holy Immortal, have mercy on us. Lord, have mercy."

She trembled again. Even with the poor light, Alexander noticed, how she turned pale and was short of breath. He embraced her and asked,

"Pray, Marie. Pray and everything will be all right, as it was earlier this morning."

Maria continued,

"O Lord Jesus Christ, Son of God, for the sake of the prayers of Thy most pure Mother and all the saints, have mercy on us. Amen."

The owners and a cook came down to the shelter when they heard the first explosions. Frau Schulenburg smiled and tried to joke,

"I am sorry, ladies and gentlemen, but they interrupted cooking breakfast for you. The Americans started to bomb not only at night but also during daytime. Their new schedule interferes with all of our schedules and plans."

Alexander asked,

"How do you know that this is American bombing and not British?"

Kurt Schulenburg answered,

"This time I saw the planes very close when they flew by in the direction of the highway. And British planes used to bomb at night."

The bombing was massive and lasted longer than half an hour. Frau Elsa said,

"It's true, now the explosions are somewhere in the area of the highway. Our troops march there. At 4 a.m., they closed the entrances to the highways. Our driver left for shopping at Erfurt and had to come back to the hotel."

The owners noticed the frightened reaction of the guests, so Mr. Schulenburg changed the topic.

"The driver came back, but we have enough food, beer, and wine to feed you."

Everyone sighed in relief.

Maria thought,

"They are good to people. They understand well that the people who stay with them at this dangerous time are in extraordinary life conditions. They lost their houses, families, and friends."

A wave of hatred for the war rose up again in Maria's mind. She whispered,

"Now the Germans suffer, paying with their lives and misfortune because of the sick cruelty of the Reich leaders. Alex, do you think they could change anything initially?"

Alexander thought for a while and answered,

"It is difficult to say, Marie. My parents could not change anything in Russia in 1917. Your father could not change anything in the Ukraine in 1940 when the same dictatorship came."

Maria watched the people around them and asked another question,

"Look, Alex, these nice people were probably initially proud of the superiority of the German nation and Nazi army?"

"Marie, my dear Marie, God had proved many times that no one could be superior but Him."

The bombing was over, and the people looked at ease because they had survived one more bombing.

The Kurbatovs extended their stay at Benedikta. They got stuck in Thüringen. They realized that there was no way to continue their driving in a southern direction. All the roads were destroyed with bombing. The German motorized units left their warped military equipment on the roads that made the movement of traffic completely impossible. There were parts of the highway with huge holes after the bombing. Alexander tried to settle Maria down,

"Marie, it was good that we were not on the road while the bombing occurred. We were lucky to stay in a cozy hotel and to have food always ready. I do not want you to lose more weight and, mon amour, you need this rest for a week in your poor condition."

Maria watched her husband with a smile.

"Alex, you talk about one week of stay in the danger and bombing in Meiningen, as if we are on vocation. Who can have rest in this tiny town that is lost in Thuringia woods?"

Alex replied without any hesitation, as if he knew it for sure,

"My love, everything is going to be fine with us. We'll pray and ask God to save us on our honeymoon trip."

Maria could not help laughing.

"Honeymoon trip! What a comparison! Do you remember about our dream to go to Italy, Spain, and Greece for our honeymoon, and to stay in each country for twelve days in the best hotels?"

"Marie, we are pretty close to the countries we dreamed about, and the hotel is not so bad, is it?"

Maria gave him a puzzled look.

"Close to what, my dear?"

Alexander answered,

"To our real honeymoon, my love."

He embraced her and covered her face and neck with kisses. She tried to cover her face from him with a hand, so he kissed her hand along with every finger and nail.

"I love you, Marie, but you are hungry and should go to breakfast now. Later I'll prove to you that this is a real honeymoon."

They laughed, as if there was no war, bombing, and death around them. Alexander picked Maria up and, holding his wife in his strong arms, started to dance. She snuggled up to him and whispered in his ear,

"I love you, Alex."

"I love you, too."

They burst into laughter again and ran to eat.

Even strong hunger did not help Maria enjoy her food.

"Alex, this is not tasty at all. May I try your dish?"

It was not tasty either.

"They waste meat and produce," Maria said.

She sighed and continued,

"One day I'll show you what I have learned to cook and bake. O, Alex, I cannot wait getting home! I am eager to prepare and feed you and your Maman with really tasty food."

Maria noticed that Alexander was thinking about something, and she did not know what it was.

"What's wrong, Alex?" she asked.

"Our tasty food will wait for a while, but you need warm clothing and this cannot wait a day," Alex replied.

It was the first rainy day at the end of September, and the temperature dropped noticeably.

Frau Elsa Schulenburg entered the dining room. Her kind and pleasant looking face had a very sad expression, though the woman tried to keep it hidden. She came up directly to Alexander and Maria,

"Do not kill the messenger, please. I have to bring you unpleasant news. All the roads going south were closed today after the second bombing. You cannot

220

move out of the town today and probably tomorrow. The armed forces were ordered to rebuild the road in order to restore traffic. I hope they'll do it quickly, but how quickly nobody knows."

Alexander answered, looking at Maria with his captivating smile,

"Well, Frau Schulenburg, we'll be your guests for a while. I hope, you do not mind."

The owner tried to smile but Maria noticed that Alexander's answer did not take away all the inner tension of Frau Schulenburg. After some hesitation, Frau Elsa delivered the second news.

"Have you seen our cook Helmut this morning? He was with us in the bomb shelter."

"Yes, we have, Frau Elsa," Maria answered.

Frau Elsa's eyes got wet with tears.

"His house was destroyed this morning during the second bombing. The whole family was buried there. My husband rushed to help him get under the ruins and to save, with God's help, his family. His neighbor said that they could hear voices there and constant cry of his baby child."

Maria exclaimed,

"O Lord! What a tragedy!"

Alexander asked,

"Where is his house, Frau Schulenburg?"

"It is in the next street, Mozart Straße, 53, one block from "Benedikta". For me, it's hard to imagine that he left his wife and three children early in the morning and lost all of them in a couple of hours."

"It is the war. Did the bomb hit the house directly?",
Alex asked.

Frau Schulenburg shook her head.

"The neighbor mentioned that the bomb exploded
somewhere close to his house; one of the walls could not
withstand the explosion and collapsed. The roof fell on
its side, destroying the front wall and burying his family
under the rubble."

Alex got excited, supposing,

"What if they are alive or at least, someone is alive.
Excuse me, ladies, but every minute is very important.
Marie, I have to run there and maybe my professional
help will be needed. The exact address is Mozart Straße
53, right?"

Alexander left.

Frau Schulenburg did not expect such a prompt
response from a new guest and honestly she told Maria,

"Who could imagine that such an elegant young
Frenchman was ready to run and help a German man
to save his family?"

Maria answered with a smile,

"That's my husband, Frau Schulenburg. Alexander
is always helpful."

Frau Schulenburg was quiet for a minute or two and
then asked Maria,

"Excuse me please, but your husband mentioned
professional help. What is he, if it is not a secret?"

"He is a surgeon."

Maria was proud of her husband. It was he, her
brave prince from a fairy tale.

Frau Elsa complained,

"I wanted to go there, as well, but today we did not find a cook to substitute Helmut. All the roads and phone lines in the area are destroyed, and no one can get here. I have to cook by myself."

Maria decided to help Frau Elsa with the preparation of food, at least on that day. She thought,

"Alex will be against my idea because he wanted me to have some rest, but that's all right. The circumstances of the day brought some changes to our plans."

Maria considered herself ready to work for half a day. She knew that morning was the most difficult time for her, so she offered to help cooking lunches and dinners with Frau Schulenburg. Frau Elsa was happy.

"God sent you to us, Marie. If two of us are in the kitchen, we have enough time to run and see what Kurt and Monsieur Alexander are doing there."

The women walked to the end of the block and turned to the right. The whole street was in ruins.

"O, my Lord! Yesterday all these houses were undamaged, and look at them now!" Mrs. Schulenburg exclaimed.

The half-destroyed home of the cook was on the opposite side of Mozart Straße, right across the street. The policemen and firefighters tried their best saving people. The ladies crossed the road and stepped onto the territory of Helmut's house. The picture was scary.

Maria looked around and found Helmut and Kurt, standing near a big firefighter near the broken window of the house. Her husband was not there. Maria got nervous. She came up to Kurt and asked,

"Excuse me, Herr Schulenburg. Where is Alexander?"

Kurt did not move his eyes from the window and answered with a low voice,

"He is inside, trying to get the people out of the basement."

Maria understood that her husband volunteered to get into the house. She did not ask any other questions and sat down on the fragment of the wall, thinking,

"Why did Alexander go in there? Why did he take such a risk? A police officer and firefighters are here. What do they wait for? Helmut knows better than anybody the construction of his house, and it is his family inside of it. Why didn't he take a risk to save them?"

Maria observed the people who were crowded near the window and realized that those old or heavy men would never reach the basement where the family stayed.

Someone near the window said softly,

"He is moving up. Help him, please."

Alexander was near a broken window and passed a child, wrapped in a quilt through the opening. The firefighter picked up the ten-month old baby, and passed him to Helmut. The boy was alive and not injured. When the baby saw his father, he smiled. Alexander did not notice Maria and disappeared again.

The tension was released a bit, and men began to talk. The old firefighter near the window raised up his hand, showing *halt*. The crowd quieted. Alexander was in the window opening again, passing another child through the window.

He had just disappeared inside, and at that moment, everyone heard a terrifying sound from the collapsing roof. It continued to cave in the middle, creating an awful noise. A five-year-old girl was frightened. The poor child was hysterical, asking her father to get into the basement and rescue their mother and brother Hanz.

Maria rushed closed and saw that the distance between the collapsed roof and floor became narrower. Everyone figured that Alexander could not crawl as quickly as before. Half an hour passed. It was an eternity for Maria. The people outside waited for him, losing patience and hope. Nobody talked. Maria came up to the window, and asked an older firefighter,

"May I go inside? Look at me; I can get into the narrowest places. I am more than sure that Alexander was stuck somewhere. I can free him, and the two of us will move forward."

Without waiting for anyone's permission, Maria turned to Helmut and asked,

"Tell me, please, in what part of the house is your basement?"

He explained quickly. Maria took off her sweater and handed the sweater to Frau Schulenburg.

Frau Schulenburg tried to stop Maria,

"Are you sure, you can help your husband?"

Maria did not answer. The people in the yard watched Maria's thin body as she slipped through the window. The policeman noticed her fragile complexion and asked out loud,

"What can she do there? How can she help that Frenchman?"

It was hard to crawl in the dust and darkness. Maria called with a low voice,

"Alex, where are you?"

She heard him answer,

"Marie, what are you doing here?"

She crawled in the direction of his voice and in a minute found him.

"Marie, help me, darling. I was caught with the belt on my back. I am afraid to pull in any direction and cannot free myself from the hook."

Maria examined the caught belt. Then she asked him to move slowly and carefully, a little bit up and backward. Alexander followed cautiously all her instructions, in order not to pull down the rest of the roof on both of them and not be buried together with his wonderful wife under the rubble. On the third try, Maria managed to release him from the hook, and they crawled forward.

"Marie, I have already found the other two bodies. Both of them are unconscious, and it is difficult for me to lift them from the basement by myself."

"Two of us can do it, mon cher." Maria answered.

She sounded determined and Alexander's hesitation disappeared. He moved faster, knowing for sure where to crawl. Then he got into the basement, without a staircase or ladder. Maria thought,

"Alexander is in good physical shape. Those old men or a big cook like Helmut would never reach the basement. Who becomes policemen and firefighters now? Most of them are elderly men who are not good for military service."

Alexander interrupted Maria's thoughts,

"Marie, I will lift the boy's body first. Pull him to the side, please, and then return to help me with his mother."

Maria did everything, as her husband expected her to do. When she returned to him, Alexander was struggling with lifting the mother of the children.

"Marie, I need a step here, otherwise I cannot lift her high enough to reach the edge of the basement and put the woman there."

"Is she alive?" Maria asked.

"Yes, Marie, but she needs to be out of here as fast as possible. She has a head trauma and the bleeding is rather strong. It's even difficult to say where she was during the explosion. Maybe the smaller kids had already been in the basement, but she and the eldest son were somewhere close to the basement at the minute of explosion. Both of them got the contusion, and she probably fell into the basement when she delivered here her unconscious son. Her head injury is rather serious."

Maria offered her help in lifting the mother of the kids.

Alexander answered,

"No, Marie. You have no strength to do it."

Then she suggested Alexander to change the position of the woman's body in his arms from horizontal to vertical so that Maria could help him lifting her. It worked. They started their crawling back out of the basement, pulling the bodies of the injured people after them. Crawling backwards made their movement slower. The frequent sounds of a creaking roof scared them. The whole house was shaking, as if it were ready to fall apart at any given moment.

Maria thought that the narrow and dark tunnel was endless. She was completely out of strength and began to pray "Our Father". In two or three minutes, they saw light. The firefighters noticed them coming and helped take out the injured people though the window. Frau Elsa rushed to Maria,

"Marichen, dear, you are so brave! My Lord, look how pale you are! Please sit down and I'll find you some cold water."

She ran to the neighbor's house across the street to ask for some cold water for Maria.

When Frau Elsa was on her way back, she saw the complete collapse of the cook's house. The woman exclaimed,

"Thank You, my Lord, for Your Holy protection of a young and wonderful couple!"

The ambulance arrived fast to take the patients from the collapsed house to the hospital. Kurt Schulenburg, cook Helmut, a group of policemen, and firefighters who were on the scene expressed their heartfelt gratitude to Alexander and Maria.

Maria felt inner trembling due to tiredness, and she could hardly walk back to the hotel. Simultaneously, she experienced happiness and joy about a new miracle of God that happened today with her husband and herself in a small German town of Meiningen.

All of a sudden, she sensed pleasant rejuvenating warmth inside that was receding the annoying trembling and restoring her strength.

Glory to Thee, o Lord! Glory to Thee!

Chapter 15

Life went on. After a short rest, the Schulenburgs and the Kurbatovs were on their way to the hotel, discussing the tragic circumstances of the day. The Schulenburgs could not stop expressing their appreciation, admiration, and surprise.

Frau Schulenburg concluded,

"The Lord brought you to us. He knew that none of us could perform what both of you got done today."

While taking a shower after their crawling in the dusty house, Maria mentioned to Alexander that she offered Frau Elsa to substitute Helmut for cooking lunches and dinners, until his wife recovered.

Alexander was concerned about Maria's health condition and replied with some nervousness in his voice,

"Marie, if you feel strong enough, then you can try it. I agree to be your driver and assistant when you need me for shopping, especially with your trips to the farmer's market and other places where the loading and unloading is required. The first moment you feel deterioration of your health due to persistent tiredness, please tell me without any hesitation."

Maria was uptight when she cooked her first lunches and dinners at "Benedikta" under the consistent attention of both owners. In a couple of days, Frau Elsa was amazed with Maria's deep knowledge of culinary art that Maria had learned at Frau Martha's Restaurant and Bakery.

Maria was appreciative for everything she learned at Frau Martha's place, but she did not want to recollect what happened at the end of her stay there. It was not her fault or the fault of those sisters. It was the war: the unpredictable, bloodcurdling, and anguishing war. It was so easy to become a victim of whimsical circumstances and to wind up in a concentration camp.

Frau Elsa was very much like Frau Marta. Both of them were tall and strong women with pleasant faces and naturally light hair. Maria liked the smiles of both women. Their smiles made them so much alike.

From that day on, the guests of the hotel "Benedikta" enjoyed everything they found in the menu. Some local people started to come for dinners and suppers, as well. Taking into consideration that the dining room was too small, the local people used to appear earlier in order to find a seat. They thanked the owners for the delicious food and pastry. It was a forgotten treat that they began allow themselves during the war.

The Schulenburgs decided not to charge the Kurbatovs' stay, and her husband began to pay the young couple some salary. The owners admitted that the additional income for October and November was so significant that it was unfair to leave Alexander and Maria without a salary. The Kurbatovs worked hard. Alexander's car could be seen near the Farmer's Market every other day. Maria kept in mind the first lesson of

Frau Martha: "Remember, Marichen, you can make a real culinary miracle only with fresh products and produce."

At the end of October 1944, one of the guests brought the news that the Soviet military forces had invaded Yugoslavia, East Prussia, and Norway. The Allies had landed in Greece. Frau Elsa was frightened to death with the news about the Russians. The American and British air forces continued persistent bombing of German cities, towns, railways, and roads where they could see the marches of German military forces. Human losses were very high, and thousands of people had lost their homes. However, the thought that the Russians would come and capture Germany was the most frightening for her, and not only for her.

Benedikta became one of the most popular places in the area. Everyone enjoyed Maria's talent in cooking and baking. Only one thing did not satisfy the visitors: the limited number of seats in the dining room. In December, before Christmas, the owners decided to renovate the restaurant and add a couple of new tables to the dining room. The guests were enthusiastic about the expansion. It took three days for Alexander and two helpers to paint the ceilings and papering the walls. The tables were positioned in a new way, and the whole place looked fresh and completely different.

Maria arranged the reopening celebration with dishes from a special menu. She was grateful to God that the farmers continued bringing fresh produce and products to the Farmers' market, where Alexander was the first to purchase them. Some farmers delivered dairy products and produce directly to Benedikta. One thing made the owners and the cook dissatisfied: it looked again that the dining place was too small and they were not able to accommodate all the comers.

Every guest of the hotel tried Maria's new dishes, and they liked them all. Frau Elsa repeated every time,

"Marie, I am sure that the Divine forces sent you to our place. I praise the Lord every day for bringing you here. *Glory to Thee, o Lord! Glory to Thee!*"

Maria smiled and replied in her thoughts,

"I know that our Lord watches us all the time and knows better what, where and when we need, but only the war could bring me to your place, Frau Elsa. It was the war, and nothing else. The war, like an unmerciful hurricane, pulled me out of my native home and dragged through my horrible German life."

Maria and Alexander acknowledged that currently, there was no possibility to leave Germany, and they were lucky to live and work in a friendly atmosphere where every guest in the town enjoyed Maria's culinary art. While working with different people, Maria noticed a very interesting phenomenon: preparations for Christmas brought people of Meiningen back to life. She mentioned it to Alexander,

"Alex, look at these people and how they live in a choking circle of war. Every day there are battles and losses, if not in Ardennes, East or West fronts, then, somewhere else. Every day, there is bombing of the German towns, cities, and roads with tremendous losses of civil population, terrible news from the fronts and Certificates of deaths on husbands, sons and fathers. Nevertheless, they are waiting for Christmas. They want to celebrate the Holy Day. They come and make reservations at *Benedikta* for Christmas lunch or dinner."

"Marie, that is wonderful!" Alex replied.

He embraced Maria and continued,

"The war did not kill the spirit of life. Are you going to make our guests happy with the Christmas delicacies? I cannot keep waiting to enjoy a traditional Christmas goose or some homemade liverwurst! Their mouths will be watering when they see such foods on their tables!"

On Christmas day, the inhabitants of the half-ruined town put on their best dresses, suits, fur coats, and hats, and went to the morning services at their churches. After the Christmas services, they enjoyed long conversations around the holiday tables at *Benedikta*.

Maria thought,

"What keeps them so alive? The war is not over, and even when it is over, it will be a complete defeat. What supports the spirit of these unfortunate people?"

She smiled and answered her question,

"Who supports us in a complete disaster? Only He can make it, our Creator, Father and Savior. At this time, God handed His hand to innocent people and made their spirit stronger."

Alexander also understood the attitude of Germans,

"People are tired of years of disaster, unmerciful deaths, and fear. They suffocated for all the years of misfortune. Fear, that *tomorrow* will not come, was killing their joy for years. That is why everyone asks God for the best Christmas gift - to take away fear and the chaos of the war from their lives. Who can blame them that now they prefer the dishonorable end to the endless suffering?"

Alexander and Maria sat in silence for a while.

Alexander added,

"Do you know what else everyone asks from God? Not to be killed at the very end of the war."

Maria agreed,

"That is understandable. Everyone wants to live. I think that all of us must cherish every moment of post war life."

Truthfully, Alexander and Maria were happy at that small hotel, where they found lodge, board, and job that gave them the possibility to wait for better times. Maria gained some weight, and they bought warm clothing for her.

Frau Elsa was happy with finding a talented chef, and she gave Maria, as a Christmas gift, some of her own expensive clothes. Maria looked gorgeous in her new dresses.

Frau Schulenburg complained, looking at Maria,

"It is difficult to imagine that a couple of years ago I was close to your size."

On Christmas night, Maria started to talk about her great desire to visit her family after the war,

"I do not know anything about them and worry a lot. Can you imagine, Alex, that the news about the bombing of our train in September of 1941 could reach my family? They might think that I've been dead since then."

Alexander advised her that a trip to the Ukraine in the near future could be dangerous.

"Marie, everything is different there after the war and who knows if you are welcomed to the country you left many years ago. Do you remember your visit in 1940? We have to wait until everything becomes clear."

Maria sighed. She agreed with Alexander's arguments,

"The soviets could take over your lands, homes, and clinic. It happened already in 1917 in Russia with my family. Then in their twenties, the same expropriation took place in eastern Ukraine. You were the witnesses of nationalization in western Ukraine in 1940, in the regions that did not belong to the Soviet Union. They used another word, but the meaning is the same, Marie. You cannot be sure that anything that belonged to count Kotyk remains to be Count Kotyk's, or that your family lives there happily. Darling, I am sorry, but I have my doubts about it."

Maria prayed a lot on behalf of her beloved. When she was praying, her heart ached, as if someone squeezed it periodically.

"Alex, promise me, please, that one day we'll go there."

She pronounced the same request in different words every time at the end of her prayers.

Alexander looked at her with love and understanding.

"Certainly, mon cher. One day we'll go there. I would like to go to Blue Creeks with you. Do you know why?"

Maria could not pick up what he had in his mind.

Alexander explained.

"I want to see your light and spacious house, Marie, with the room on the second floor where my love was born and grew up. I want to wander with you, mon amour, hand-in-hand, in the emerald meadows and forests that you vividly described so many times when we were students."

Maria watched him with surprise. Alexander continued.

"I want to smell the wild flowers and touch the Ukrainian silky grass that made my wife's hair sweet, fragrant, and silky."

Alexander embraced Maria and smelled her hair. Maria smiled and wanted to say something but Alexander did not want to be interrupted.

"I want to swim with you in the river that is cool, even during the hottest days of the summer. I want to sleep with you in your beautifully hand carved bed. I want to sit with you at night on the balcony and observe the velvet of the sky with the diamond stars in it. I want us to change the spirit of the whole house, where your father was so lonely for many years. We'll fill it with our pure love."

Maria looked at her husband with admiration. He remembered every detail of her description that she told him years ago. Even the war did not erase it from his memory. She snuggled up to him. Alexander picked her up and put her on the bed, covering her face, neck, and hands with kisses.

"I love you, Marie. I am ready to die for you at any moment, but I want to live a long life, watching the lives of our children and grandchildren. I want you to be happy and joyful again. Trust me, Marie: I will always love you."

She played with him:

"Oh no, my darling, I do not believe in your eternal love. When I turn old and ugly, you will not love me at all."

Maria burst into laughing. It was a moment when she was overwhelmed with happiness and she could not stop saying nonsense and laugh at it again.

Glory to Thee, o Lord! Glory to Thee!

Chapter 16

The flow of customers at Benedikta increased rapidly after the celebration of the winter holidays - Christmas and the New 1945 Year. One day in the middle of January, Maria suggested to the owners that they hire one more cook for the preparation of lunches and dinners "to go."

She explained,

"The income from a new part of the restaurant business will help you save some money for purchasing the next door space and to build a big restaurant on the first floor with wide and nicely decorated glass windows, while reconstructing the second floor space of the kitchen and dining room into additional guest rooms."

Frau Elsa liked the idea very much and in two days, a new cook was working in the kitchen side-by-side with Maria, learning her culinary art. It took a little bit longer than two weeks, and those inexpensive but freshly made and tasty meals became popular among the residents of Meiningen. Two boys delivered them on their bicycles, making some money and food for their families with many other children. They tried to substitute for their fathers, who were killed at the beginning of the war. The boys looked serious and were very responsible at just twelve years of age. The war destroyed their childhood and made them adults ahead of time.

Watching those wonderful boys every day and feeding them in the kitchen, Maria started to think frequently about a child. Alexander and she did not do anything to prevent a pregnancy. She decided to talk to her husband about her worries.

One day she came up to Alexander and said with a very concerned facial expression, as she was going to take an exam. He remembered that face, when she was a student:

"I need to talk to you, Alex."

Alexander smiled and wanted to embrace his wife but she moved back and asked:

"Please, sit down. It is a serious topic to discuss."

Alexander was going to sit in an armchair when she asked:

"What do you think about a child, Alex?"

"About what, I mean, what I think about who? Excuse me, Marie, but I am completely lost."

"I mean, what do you think about our child, my dear? I constantly catch myself at the thought that I want to get pregnant with your child, but I am afraid of it."

"What are you afraid of, my darling?"

"I am afraid of having a child, because of the war and my physical exhaustion. You know well, Alex that a child cannot be strong when a mother is weak."

Alexander rushed toward his wife, picked her up and kissed her. His answer sounded not as an answer of a physician, but a loving husband.

"Mon amour, God will bless us with our son when you are strong again. Marie, I want you to know one thing: whenever it happens, I will be the happiest man in the whole world."

"Alex, I believe you, and I want to make you happy."

The thought about a child was strong and persistent. Maria recollected the words of her father about children. One day, she had assisted him with two child deliveries and he shared his understanding with Maria. Two infants were born in different physical conditions. He told her,

"All children are blessed by God when they are conceived with love."

Being a physician, her father mentioned a fact that was obvious for him and proved by his wide experience: the child that was conceived and born with the love of the parents and grandparents, was stronger and developed faster in comparison with an "unwished" or "accidental" child.

Maria doubted this and decided to check her father's theory. Her father was absolutely right. In one family, the strong boy was the third child. The family was happy to have him, and everyone awaited his birth joyfully. In the second case, it was the second child, but the mother did not want to have him at all.

One day Maria heard what Dr. Kotyk mentioned to two colleagues,

"The parents, especially mothers, are sinners when they do not want their children to be born. We have no right to destroy anything that is blessed from above.

My patients know my definite and unchangeable opinion about this matter and do not disturb me with anything except the observation of the pregnancy and child delivery. I believe that all children come into this world for higher purposes. Who are we to destroy God's objectives?"

Maria was grateful to God for being born in love. Whatever happened later did not affect her development during her mother's pregnancy. Ten years of her life in a loving family made Maria the happiest among four children. She remembered her mother very well: her classically beautiful face with large hazel eyes, her calm voice, her long dark braids, and especially her mother's hands with diamond or pearl rings on her long, delicate fingers. Maria remembered her mother's hands, when her mother played piano or taught Maria to play.

Maria missed her mother her entire life. One day she told Alexander,

"By the way, Alex, my Maman Anna, left one diamond ring for me at the moment of her departure. She loved me very much. I remember her clearly, as if she left yesterday. When the carriage waited for Maman to take her to the railway station, she tried not to cry, hugging, and kissing all of her children. But the separation was not easy for any of us."

Maria paused for a minute and then continued.

"I was shocked when she came up to our father and kneeled. Mamma asked,

'Forgive me, Lukian. Please, forgive me and do not curse. I do not want my new child to pay for my sins."

"Marie, how was your father? What was his reaction at such a confession?"

"Papa rushed to her, picked her up, and kissed her gently, touching her hair with his hands from both sides of the hat. Then he stepped back and said,

"I love you, Anna, and sincerely wish you God's blessing for your new life. You have my word: I would never curse your choice."

Alexander realized that it was necessary for Maria to release the memories of her mother. He asked a question in order to change the painful topic,

"Where is your engagement ring, Marie?"

"I left it at home, but who knows where it is now."

Maria returned again to the previous topic,

"By the way, I tried to wear my mother's engagement ring many times. The pure diamond in the size of four carats sparkled brightly with different colors. I tried to wear it after graduation from monastery school. It was my size, but I felt some kind of heaviness in the ring and the heaviness did not allow me to enjoy it. Maybe my mother's pain was left in it, who knows?"

Maria sighed deeply.

"Papa wanted me to have it after our engagement. The war screwed up everything."

Maria looked at her husband. Then she blessed herself with a cross and said,

"Thank you, God that we love each other and are happy together, even during the war!"

She smiled and pronounced the rest of the prayer in a low voice.

"Dear God, bless my husband with a son, whenever Thee consider the right time for us."

The war events in January and February of 1945 were appalling for the German nation; Nazis withdrew from Ardennes, and the German attacks were completely eliminated at all the fronts. The battered troops were moving slowly along the ruined roads under the bombing of the Allies. The Soviet army captured Warsaw, Poznan, and Danzig. On February 6, 1945, their troops settled down at the other side of the river Oder.

The Allies captured Saarbrucken. On February 13, Dresden was burned down with an incendiary raid of Allies, with huge number of civilian losses. Everyone understood that the end of the war was close. The Nazi army did not have strength any more. It was totally destroyed while suffering defeat during the last battle in Ardennes.

It was time when German people arose in the morning and were not sure if they would see again their friends, neighbors, or even family members who lived next door, in the next street, or another town. It was seldom, when their sleep was not interrupted at night with the sounds of sirens, rumble of planes, whistling and bomb explosions. It was a miracle when they did not need to pick up the babies and children out of their beds and to run toward the nearest bomb shelters. Every day Maria thanked God in her morning prayers for keeping them alive.

The working day of Maria and Alexander usually started at 6:00 in the morning and was over at 10:00 at night. The restaurant was always busy, and their salaries were way up in comparison with the initial month. Maria did not complain, but the owners saw that it was already getting impossible for Maria to cook three meals a day without professional assistance. This was due to significantly increased number of guests. They hired one more cook to help Maria for preparation of dinners and suppers, besides the one who was dealing just with the orders to go.

The Kurbatovs could not wait for the end of the war. They earned some money, but this was of no interest to them; the bombing of the Allies pulled down the houses, stores, libraries, and museums. If they even wanted to buy a house or an apartment to live and continue for a while their work at Benedikta, there was nothing in the area. Who could take a risk investing money in a house under the threat of everyday bombing?

The Schulenburgs wanted the Kurbatovs to be their partners for a new restaurant project. Maria mentioned it to her husband,

"The Creator allows people to dream even during the war. I made some suggestions to Frau Elsa and to my mind she liked them."

"What did you suggest, Marie?"

Maria answered, with some shyness in her voice,

"Do you remember the castle hotel in Gottingen that impressed me so much?"

"Marie, what is so similar between the castle and this regular building?"

"A lot," Maria replied.

Everyday, the two women had the opportunity to discuss the construction project while working together in the kitchen. When they figured out what could be realistically done, both of them were in love with it. They wanted their husbands to like the project as well and to be involved in it.

Maria had volunteered to prepare a description and calculations for the big project, which consisted of two parts. The first part of the project included details for remodeling of the existing hotel. It included considerable hall reconstruction, as well as conversion of the kitchen, two spacious walking closets, and the dining room into additional guest rooms. She came to a decision to describe in detail to the owners, as she saw it. It took a week to prepare such a plan. It was great that the second cook was good enough to pick up Maria's instructions quickly, and he was able to work in the kitchen by himself, so that Maria could spent more time with the project.

The second part of the project included the description of the new restaurant construction, which was planned to operate not only for the guests of *Benedikta*, but other customers, as well. Maria aimed at proof that a new restaurant should not be detached from the hotel building, as a separate construction. On the contrary, it should be structurally attached to the entrance hall, and be exposed to all the hotel residents. Maria planned to arrange high quality room service.

She wanted everyone to get the message that the remodeling and construction required a lot of work and assets. Maria and Alexander agreed to invest all the money they had earned earlier into the project in order to make Benedikta one of the most popular places, and not only in Meiningen, but in the whole Germany.

"We should not build a regular hotel. We should build a castle, similar to the one we stayed in Gottingen. It should be one of the best jewels of hospitality business in Thüringen and Europe."

Everyone listened to Maria with great interest. The gentle, slightly pale, but absolutely beautiful young lady, dressed in an elegant light gray suit and black shoes was full of interesting ideas as well as wonderful and prosperous projects. It seemed as if all the projects jumped out of her enormously large, hazel eyes. The project she described looked miraculous but do-able. She had God's inspiration and special feeling inside. It seemed, she spread that inspiration, removing all fears and doubts.

After naming all of the objectives, Maria began the detailed description of the works that they had to organize. Using a big sheet of brown wrapping paper, Maria made several drawing as to how she saw the remodeling of the existing entrance hall. She hung the drawing on the wall and commented,

"An entrance hall is a very important place at any hotel. We should invest significant assets in remodeling it with light marble floors, an attractive fountain, and statues. At the end of the hall, we should build beautiful marble staircases, which lead into two opposite directions to the guest suites on the second floor. The stairs should be also made of marble material with golden rails, but lighter in color than the floors of the hall. The stairs should look like two wings of a big bird, taking guests to a pleasant flight."

Maria was interrupted by Mr. Schulenburg's question.

"Marie, I am sorry for the interruption, but what lighting do you think we need for such an entrance hall?"

Maria smiled,

"From the ceiling of the second floor, right in the middle of the hall there will be a magnificent chandelier with multiple crystal layers and cascades. On the walls between the statues we'll hang small crystal lights as well."

Maria thought, "I wish we could have the chandelier from my mother's family castle."

She called to mind the next important idea and said,

"The elevator should be installed behind the staircases. Many people were wounded during the war and would not be able to use the stairs to get to their suites."

Frau Elsa exclaimed,

"Great, Marie! You are so considerate. Presently, we have several guests whose houses were destroyed, and they were injured. Every time, these people have a problem to get down to the bomb shelter and to return to their rooms."

The future partners started the discussion about a new restaurant. They understood the necessity to build a two-storied addition that would be connected with the renovated hall. At the same time, the new restaurant would have two separate entrances for the public: one entrance directly from the street, and another entrance from a parking lot through a summer café.

Maria noticed,

"By the way, we'll put only round tables in the restaurant and café. A party of five people can easily sit at a round table."

She stopped for a minute, looked at her audience, and made a conclusion.

"The Schulenburgs will purchase a construction lot for the new restaurant and additional ten guest rooms on the second floor. The Kurbatovs decided to buy the next space for an outside summer café and a large parking lot."

Alexander added,

"The whole block of the street will belong to Benedikta. Isn't that impressive?"

Maria continued with her calculations. She operated easily with estimates, numbers, and terms, as if it was not the first project in her life. Elsa and Kurt Schulenburg listened to Maria with respect. What an interesting personality she had! The graduate from one of the most famous medical schools, she cooked and baked as no other professional they had met for seventeen years of their business. Right now, she sounded much like an experienced business woman who had been in the hospitality business for at least a decade.

Both Schulenburg thought, "It is a miracle that God brought her to our place."

When Maria had finished the presentation of the new project, she took a seat, looking at her audience with inquiry and impatience. All three of them were speechless for a while. She smiled, looked at the clock and asked,

"I made you tired for an hour and twenty minutes, did I? Maybe, you found the project very expensive? I agree. Nonetheless, we need a castle with statues and fountains, with real paintings and crystal lighting. We need a real castle for our hospitality business that will attract paying guests from everywhere."

Alexander was the first who came up and kissed his wife.

"Thank you, Marie, for your clear vision of this project and explicable and meticulous presentation. You are my miracle, darling!"

Frau Elsa hugged Maria with words of gratitude for her brilliant mental picture of their future mutual business. They decided to celebrate on that day. The cooks, well-trained by Maria, were working by themselves, serving the guests and their owners.

Everyone saw that the owners sat together with the Kurbatovs around the corner table with a bottle of French wine, discussing or celebrating something that made all of them excited and happy.

The new partners were not only celebrating. Other than that, they worked on a plan of action. Those actions, with God's blessing, might lead them to success, happiness, and prosperity. All of them were full of life. They did not remember when they had last experienced such an uplifting. It was so long ago that none of them could recall it. Even the hotel guests had noticed that evening that there was something unusual in the behavior of the normally calm people.

Mr. Schulenburg noticed,

"It is funny, when four people in the middle of the war are planning the construction of a magnificent castle for guests and further growth of the hospitality business. Isn't it wonderful?"

He suggested a toast,

"To our mutual success."

Frau Elsa was the first who looked, as if she woke up from dreaming and asked,

"Why are we doing this now? There is war everywhere, and tomorrow we could 'move' into another world."

Her cautious phrase interrupted their vivid conversation. They sat in silence for a couple of minutes, looking at each other. Maria smiled and said in her usual gentle voice,

"We are not crazy, Frau Elsa. The war is coming to its end. We are part of the nature. The hurricane of war did not destroy us and we, as the trees, begin to shoot stronger closer to springtime. The Creator blesses us with new plans, thoughts, dreams, and the ways of their realization."

"Maybe you are right, Marie," Frau Elsa replied. "We are tired to think about war, danger, and death. God knows what to do and when."

Alexander and Maria revealed their dream that with time, they planned on leaving Germany and returning to their medical practice in Paris. The money they intended currently to invest into the hospitality business would allow them to support the building of their own clinic in the future.

Frau Elsa asked,

"Would you like to build your own clinic in Germany?"

Alexander looked at Maria and answered,

"Quite possibly."

It was strange for Maria to hear such a reply, and her big eyes became bigger. She remembered the time when he was the one who did not want to go anywhere away from Paris.

Maria asked,

"How come, my darling?"

Alexander replied,

"Maybe it is difficult to understand, Marie, but I was blessed with my personal happiness here in Germany. The sense of happiness has changed my attitude. People must live in the places where they are happy. Patients are everywhere. They need us, doctors, in every country. The war is not over, and it is too early to discuss this matter. I believe that God will put everything and everyone in the right place and make all the corrections."

He turned to Elsa and Kurt and said,

"Do you know why we are with you now? You are honest and nice people. We'll be happy to be your friends and partners."

They toasted to friendship and successful partnership. The last toast was the most important. Kurt pronounced it in a low voice,

"To the end of the war."

On Thursday, the Schulenburgs successfully purchased the space next door. A new lot was acquired for a low price, and they saved enough money to do some pre-construction job. Alexander and Maria decided not to waste time and buy another nearby lot for the summer café and parking lot. Signing the purchase agreement was the easiest thing. People of the ruined houses were happy to get some money to live.

Glory to Thee, o Lord! Glory to Thee!

Chapter 17

At the end of March, the entire western front was east of the Rhine River. On April 1, 1945, the US armies linked up to cut off more than 300,000 troops of Nazi armies in the Ruhr. By April 14, the American troops spliced the "kettle" of the Ruhr, and US army reached the Elbe River, south of Magdeburg. The US troops captured southern Bayern and Nurnberg by April 17.

The owners and guests of Benedikta did not know what to expect from the Allies, but most of them experienced constant fear of the occupation by Russian troops. Frau Elsa used to ask nearly every day,

"What should we do with our plans and life if Russians come?"

Alexander was optimistic.

"We should live our life. They would not stay here forever. The moment they leave, we would start the construction of Benedikta's Castle. Am I right?"

Everybody liked the new name of the hotel.

"But when will they leave, if they hadn't come yet?" Kurt asked impatiently.

Alexander parried a question,

"Were you expecting them at a definite date and time, and they did not show up, Herr Schulenburg?"

"Not me," Kurt answered.

They tried to push away worries and fears. They kept joking, but their jokes did not alleviate the mutual tension. The partners realized that they were unable to sit without doing anything. Expectations that something good, bad, or nothing could happen to them did not work. Their wives were preoccupied with cooking everyday meals.

The next day after buying the lots, Alexander and Kurt together with three helpers started clearing of a space for their new restaurant. They had to demolish and remove the remains from the previous constructions, preparing the space for a new addition. Both men had not performed much physical work in their lives, but it was nonsense to waste money hiring somebody else just for clearing off a space. They decided to finish this work by the end of the war.

Every evening Alexander was very tired. He refused to have dinner or their traditional evening tea. Maria was smart when she arranged nutritious snacks for men at five o'clock. They worked from sunrise to sunset. When Alexander came home after work, he took a shower and fell asleep faster than his head touched the pillow.

Maria liked to sit for some time next to her sleeping husband. She used to put some cream on his hands and massaged them gently. She felt sorry for Alexander, caringly kissed him and whispered,

"My poor Count, you would never be involved in such work if not for the war and if not for me. You came here to save me and to bring me back to life. You made me happy again, and you returned my desire to create and to make other people happy. Thank you, mon amour!"

Maria kissed him lovingly and added,

"Thank You, Lord, for everything!"

Alexander answered,

"You are welcome, darling."

Maria smiled at his answer. Alexander was asleep and smiled in his dreams. His face looked calm and very handsome. Maria kissed him and pronounced the words that delivered the most important message of her heart.

"I love you, darling. I am so happy with you."

He answered with his sleepy voice,

"I love you too, Marie. I…"

Before going to bed, Maria prayed a lot for both of them, her family in the Ukraine, Alexander's mother in France, and her mother somewhere in Canada. She thanked God for the day and everything that had happened during that nice day. At the end of her prayers, the light and warmth that was so familiar for her, but lost for a while, appeared again in Maria's body.

"Glory to Thee, O Lord. Glory forever," Maria said quietly.

Maria felt sorry for Alexander, but she knew from her own experience that with time the human body could adapt to any work. That happened to her years ago. She transformed into an enduring woman from a fragile girl. Her father could hardly imagine his daughter feeding, washing, milking cows, cleaning the barn and carrying heavy buckets or pushing a heavy cart with produce and dairy products for five miles every morning and then cooking and baking in the heat of the kitchen, or standing for long hours in the operating room, assisting the surgeons.

"Thank you, my Lord for giving us endurance, patience, and will-power when we need it."

Kurt and Alexander were happy to volunteer their strength, intensive work, and time for the future mutual business. Both gentlemen were very proud of themselves when the cleansing cycle was over. They collected all the fragments in the corner of their future parking lot. The place for a new construction was sizeable, and they saw what they could build there with time. The customers could reach their place from three different streets, and accessibility was always beneficial for any business.

Maria liked the persistence of her husband. She thought,

"My Papa would hardly recognize both of us. The war had changed us greatly."

The thought about her father pricked her heart. He had not heard anything about her for four years, but he could find the information about train bombings, fires, and unmerciful execution.

"The news about my terrible death could keep my father in suffering and kill my grandpa," Maria thought.

Maria decided to find the possibility of getting in touch with her family. She mentioned to Frau Elsa,

"After the war I'll go there for a week, just to see them all, and to find out how they are doing."

The next morning she talked to Alexander about her decision to contact her family. In general, he did not have anything against it. The only thing he asked her was,

"Marie, you have to postpone any contacts until the war is over. You have to be certain that there is no mutual danger for your family in the Ukraine from having contact with you and for you, visiting them in Creeks."

On April 23, the Russian army entered Berlin, and in two days, American and Russian forces met at Torgau on the Elbe River. Those were the last weeks of the war. The world learned the terrible facts about the inhuman tortures in the Nazi concentration camps. The first concentration camps were built in Germany when Hitler's regime came to power. The very first one was built in 1933 near Munich, in a suburban part of a small town Dachau.

In 1937, the Nazis had built a Buchenwald concentration camp near Weimar with its world famous sign over the entrance: "Jedem das Seine", that meant – *"To each his own"*. Weimar is a famous German town, known for centuries for its cultural life. Goethe, Schiller, Franz List, and Bach lived in Weimar. Between July 1937 and April 1945, some 250,000 people were incarcerated in Buchenwald. The sick Nazi regime murdered 56,000 inmates only at Buchenwald.

About 14,000 concentration camps were built in Germany and other countries occupied by Nazis, where inmates underwent inhuman tortures, exploitation, starvation, execution in gas cameras, and incineration in crematoriums. The civilized population of the earth learned about uncivilized conditions of Colditz, Bergen Belsen, Dora Mittelbau, Auschwitz, Mauthausen, and others.

The sickening facts and obscenity of the Holocaust were revealed to mankind. Auschwitz-Birkenau, Chelmno, Belzec, Treblinka, Sobibor and Majdanek in Poland were established by Nazis to "finalize the problem with Jews and Polish, communists and clergy, scientists and writers, etc."

May 8, 1945 was declared in Europe as Victory Day. Germany was subdivided into four zones of occupation: American, Russian, British, and French. The population of Germany was expecting new changes in their lives. Thüringen belonged to the Russian zone of occupation.

Frau Elsa repeated constantly,

"I do not want to stay here. We should leave for Wurzburg."

Kurt and Alexander tried to calm her down, but the poor woman did not want to run her business in a Russian zone. Maria was against staying under the Soviet occupation, as well. She remembered the terrible process of nationalization in Western Ukraine,

"I am not sure, gentlemen, that the hotel we plan to construct in the Russian zone, will belong to us in future. I doubt it."

The war was over, but the problems in their lives were not resolved. Maria was afraid to stay in Meiningen, but the Kurbatovs did not have money to move anywhere else. All the money they made was invested in the construction lot.

Maria started to write letters to her father. She had sent dozens of them, but did not receive an answer. Then she wrote a letter to her cousin in Krakow. It was a big surprise to her when she received an answer in twenty days! Her cousin described the events that Maria was unable to understand and believe. She read the informative letter of her cousin many times, and then read it to Alexander, asking him to explain to her what her cousin tried to reveal there.

The cousin wrote,

"They – Russian troops – arrived to your grandfather mansion, beat him, and threw the old man out of his house. Somebody saw him living in the woods. Presently, it is very dangerous to live in the woods, because the fighters of Organization of Ukrainian Nationalists and Ukrainian Insurgent Army are still there, and NKVD conducts the numberless operations against UPA and OUN.

Nobody had heard anything about your father, Marie and nobody had seen your father since last spring when the soviets appeared at your mansion. They occupied your house, and he disappeared. I understand that you worry a lot about your family. Sorry Marie, but I cannot write anything cheering that will pacify you.

People who ran away from soviets to Poland told us, that your brothers were taken somewhere, supposedly to Russia for force labor and studies. Marie, I have also learned that the soviets took Jenny to the orphanage and labor. I do not know, Marie, where your siblings are now. I hope that the Lord is merciful on them and they are alive and healthy.

The soviets expropriated all the lands, forests, factories, banks and houses of Ukrainian nobility. So, we do not have anything there, everything belongs to the soviets."

Maria questioned,

"What country does everything belong to? Russia? It cannot be!"

She continued reading the letter,

"I beg you, Marie not to go home. Stay where you are. We also have no idea what to expect from a new regime in Poland. Russian army and NKVD continue arresting, imprisonment and executions. They destroyed our resistance movement – Polish Armia Krajowa. They have murdered hundreds of Polish and Ukrainian patriots from OUN and UPA and presently, the NKVD continues its annihilative operations in the forests and villages of Western Ukraine and Poland. I beg you, Marie, do not go back! Remember, they are atrocious."

Maria's cousin underlined the last sentence three times. The next sentence clarified everything,

"I am sorry, dear, but we do not have our homes there."

Maria felt disturbed,

"She wants me not to go there. How do you like it, Alex? My father disappeared, my brothers and poor Jenny were taken somewhere to Russia, and my Grandpa is probably dying due to starvation in the woods. I have to go there, as soon as possible. I have to find my family and bring all of them to France."

Alexander and the Schulenburgs were not so enthusiastic about Maria's trip to the Ukraine. Maria did not want to discuss it with them, seeing an absence of support in their wish to stop her, and blaming them in callousness to some extend in such an important matter.

One day she said,

"All of you are afraid of mysterious enemies which my cousin mentioned in her letter. I have no idea about OUN, UPA, and NKVD. I do not want to be in contact with any of them. I will go there to find my family and to help them to leave for France, as soon as possible. Nobody can stop me here or there."

Maria wrote a letter to a Russian consulate in Berlin. She explained in her letter that the Nazis sent her to Germany for force labor and she had to work on the farm and later, as a cook and baker. Thank God, Alexander did not allow her to mention her work at the military hospital. She asked the commandant of the Russian zone for permission to enter the country in order to find her family. She did not want anything except taking her family to France.

Maria could not keep waiting for an answer. The Kurbatovs received their new passports from France. Every day she checked the mailbox, but the answer from the Russian administrative office was not there. The long expectation did not diminish Maria's desire to go to the Ukraine. It was nice that Maria was very busy and her attention was distracted from it during daytime. The

Kurbatovs saw one another only at night. No matter how tired she was, she did not go to sleep without touching on the topic about the visit of her family. Maria prayed at night, asking God to give her the possibility to visit her family and to take them away from the dangerous country. Sometimes it seemed like an obsession.

It was the spring of 1946, the first spring after the war. Maria liked this season of the year. It was nature's awaking after its winter sleep. Some days were very warm, and their warmth allowed new leaves and flowers to shoot and bloom. The days became longer, and Maria started to walk with Alexander every evening, as they used to do it in France a long time ago. Sometimes the Schulenburgs accompanied them. They discussed their plans for the next day, week, or month.

They decided to postpone the construction of the new addition, because they were not sure that they could own "Benedikta castle" under the new regime. The land was purchased, but nobody wanted to take a risk and invest in construction that could be expropriated any day.

Alexander presumed,

"If they decide to take away the lots, we partially lose our money. If they take away the castle, we lose everything."

The partners made the decision to renovate the existing building. They installed the elevator and started to work on transferring the restaurant and kitchen to the basement, the former bomb shelter.

Alexander and Kurt hired several house painters to work on the ceiling and walls. They brought two other men to paper the walls with beautiful wallpaper. The new doors to the restaurant were hand carved and looked very impressive when the elevator opened in basement.

The work on the new restaurant was completed in two weeks. They hung three large and seven small crystal chandeliers. Nothing should remind their guests that once it was a bomb shelter. The owners furnished it with round tables and elegant armchairs. Crispy white tablecloths brought additional light to the room.

The Schulenburgs planned initially to transfer the appliances of the old hotel kitchen to a new one. Maria made another suggestion: to install a brand new, modern type kitchen, because the old one was used enough for disassembling and installing in a new place. In a week a new shiny kitchen was delivered and installed. This kitchen included three stoves and two ovens. It means that a chef and three cooks could work simultaneously at different dishes without waiting for each other. Mr. Schulenburg still worried,

"A new restaurant had to bring sufficient income in order to cover at least part of our expenses for the hotel renovation."

Maria noticed,

"The speed of hotel renovation means a lot. We cannot do it for several months. One month is good enough to complete the partial reconstruction."

"I am not sure that all the work can be done during one month. Even partial reconstruction requires time," Kurt Schulenburg replied.

Alexander suggested,

"As long as we need it to be done quickly, we have to hire not one but two construction teams. We'll spend more money, but win time."

All of them knew that no one could check in and stay in the hotel during the reconstruction. So, two teams of workers were hired for speedy job in order to complete the renovation and furnishing in a month.

Part of Maria's dreams came true – the presentable entrance hall with light marble floors, statues, and small crystal lights was ready to meet new guests. A spacious elevator was built behind the stairs.

However, some very important details were still missing. They did not buy a large chandelier, as Maria described in the project, and there was no fountain, exotic trees and hibiscus bushes in the center of the hall. The old one-sided stairs were not reconstructed into two-sided light marble wings-like structure. Their new central chandelier was beautiful, but not as in "Maman castle." The Schulenburgs were cautious,

"Anything extraordinary could attract the objectionable attention of the new regime. We should avoid it for now."

All the works connected with renovation, reconstruction and remodeling of the hotel came to an end on time, and the owners wanted to celebrate the grand opening on Easter in April, 1946. The new restaurant was accommodated with sixty tables. It was ten times larger than their former dining room. Three cooks besides the chef were working at Easter dinner. Frau Elsa insisted in Maria's supervision but not cooking on that day.

"Dear Marie, you have worked enough in the kitchen, as a cook and baker. Now it is the turn of your students. The holiday dinner and supper will be their test."

"I got used that you, Frau Elsa were in a position of supervisor in the kitchen."

Frau Elsa replied,

"The Easter dinner is not a regular dinner, Marie. It is Grand opening of our freshly done place. I wish we can satisfy all our guests, and four of us should meet them in our renovated entrance hall."

Maria continued,

"I know that our guests missed such a party for many years during the war. I believe, they will enjoy everything from the spacious entrance hall, where the beautiful trays with Ester breads and multicolored eggs will meet them, to our party at a spanking new restaurant."

Frau Elsa looked around and remarked,

"I hope that our guests will enjoy our Easter decorations and furnishing of the restaurant, delicious food, wines and beer, wonderful music and singers, but most of all – the unique atmosphere in Benedikta."

Since the successful Easter dinner, Maria was not working so hard in the kitchen, as she used to do. On weekdays, the partners subdivided the cooks' hours into two shifts. She supervised only one shift, while Frau Elsa supervised the other. To Maria's great surprise, she worked less intensive but was sleepy every morning, and wanted to stay in bed a bit longer.

"Why is it so that I am constantly sleepy from hardly even working in comparison with the previous year? All I want is sleep."

Maria had a suspicion,

"Maybe I feel like this due to my persistent worries about my family? Alexander is right: I am too nervous about getting the entrance documents to the Ukraine. It drained my strength."

The thoughts about her family were so unremitting that they did not allow Maria to concentrate on her life with Alexander. She could not make a decision where to go first: to France or to the Ukraine. One year passed after the end of the war, but they did not go to France and did not visit Alexander's mother. Maria said,

"Alex, I am afraid that the moment we leave for France, they would issue and deliver the visas, and if they try to deliver the documents and do not find us, we could lose the opportunity to visit my family in the Ukraine. We have to stay here and wait. We talk to your mother twice a week and, thank God, she is quite all right."

It was strange. Maria prayed, but did not get inner warmth and light for a long time, since she had sent the first request to the Russian consulate. She was surprised.

"I do not do anything wrong, did I? Where is the warmth and light? The war is over and maybe I do not need the God's guidance and support in the absence of life danger?"

Maria did not find it necessary to focus her attention on the lost connection with the Universe. She made her own decisions without concentrating on rightness.

One morning she felt sick, and the sickness bothered her for an hour. Later that day she felt great and could be seen everywhere in their renovated building. Maria blamed their newly painted hotel room for her morning sickness.

"I was inhaling the smell of paint for a week and feel nauseous due to intoxication."

The next morning, Maria vomited. Alexander asked her not to go to work. He talked to Frau Elsa. The question that Frau Elsa asked was so natural that it was difficult for two physicians not to understand from the very beginning the true reason of Maria's feeling unwell in the morning, and then feeling wonderful the rest of the day.

Alexander ran back to their room, hugged his wife, and suggested to examine her right at that moment.

Maria answered,

"My dear doctor, this morning, I have also understood what is going on. You should not examine me. Go to work, and I'll be there pretty soon."

They were happy. Alexander embraced Maria and started dancing with her around the room.

"Alex, let me go. I feel more nauseated from spinning around."

"Mon cher, all three of us are dancing together for the first time. Thank you, my love. Thank you for making me happy. I love you, Marie. If you only know how I love you!"

Alexander let Maria go. She was dizzy and had to sit down.

"I love you too, darling. However, we have to work. Go, I'll be there in five minutes."

The only problem that interfered with the news and diminished their joy and happiness was the trip to the Ukraine. Both of them thought about it but at the moment, none of them wanted to discuss it.

After two months, Maria's condition was balanced, and she did not even notice any negative signs of her pregnancy. She became an executive director of one of the best hotels and restaurants in town. Maria was great with managing their business, and management made her very excited. They were blessed that the soviet-like regime had not expropriated *Benedikta*. Not yet.

Maria was extremely busy, trying to combine the managing of the hotel, supervision in the kitchen, and preparation to become a mother. Being well-organized and proficient, she did it successfully. Maria elaborated her special "Schedule for a mother-to-be." She ate small meals every three hours, walked for 15 minutes after each meal, and took a one-hour break at 1 p.m. for lunch and half-hour sleep. She was enjoying her condition and, most of all, she enjoyed her husband's love and care for her. He was ready to do anything that would make Maria happy.

In order to prove Maria his care about her feelings to the lost family, he sent a letter to the Russian consulate with a request to allow both of them to visit the Ukraine in order to find his wife's relatives.

Maria was happy with his decision,

"I knew from the very beginning that you would accompany me. You would never let me go there alone, especially in my present condition.

The Kurbatovs were ready to go to the Ukraine during the summer, but the entry documents were delivered in September. They were a little bit confused, signing the certificate of the delivered mail. Maria was five months pregnant. She was panicky.

"Oh my God! What shall we do, Alex? If we wait for our child to come, there is no way for us to travel with him. And the travel documents will expire at the end of December."

"Marie, are you going to take a risk and travel now in your condition?"

Alexander was against their trip in the autumn of 1946. With his understanding, they could be ready to travel no earlier than in a year.

"Now we need to write a letter to Russian administrative office and explain the reason why we are not able to enter the Ukraine in the nearest time. I am sure, they will find the reason serious enough and make the extension of the documents. On that time schedule, we could take the baby to France and leave him with my mother and a babysitter."

He brought many arguments up to Maria, but she did not want to pay attention to them. Stubbornness, that was unknown before, made Maria close-minded.

"Alex, I cannot live, sleep, eat, and be totally happy when my beloved are suffering there. You have to understand me. I have never been selfish. I wanted everyone to be happy in the whole world, even my mother, who brought so much bitterness in our lives, especially in the life of our father. My darling, I need to find them, to bring them here, arrange the opportunity for my father to enjoy his grandson, and all his children around him. It's his time to be warmed with our love and respect."

Alexander had a strong feeling that on whatever his wife insisted sounded, as an obsession. At the same time, he also experienced grate pettiness and sorrow for her and her family. From the very beginning, he picked out something dangerous in the venture of visiting the Ukraine, but he was unable to stop his wife. His arguments were not strong enough, and some of them Maria refused to comprehend at all. She cried days and nights, and such stress was not healthy for either her or their baby.

By the end of September, the Kurbatovs were ready for departure. They purchased the train tickets from Berlin to Lvov for Wednesday, September 25, 1946. In Brest, during a long stop, the NKVD authorities checked the passports and the entry documents. The young officer read their entry paper with curiosity and surprise,

"The present document is issued to Count and Countess Kurbatov..."

He read it out loud twice to his partners and returned the paper to Alexander. The young couple continued their trip to Lvov.

There were few civilian passengers on the train, and those few kept the compartment doors closed at all times. The unpleasant, slimy feeling of danger did not allow Maria to enjoy her journey. She felt angry with herself,

"Alex, why do people change their desires so easily?"

Alexander asked with a smile,

"You mean people in general, or just you, darling?"

She did not answer his question. Alexander smiled, but Maria did not see joyfulness in his eyes. He was unusually tense.

The young woman wished to cancel this trip for time-being and not travel in her condition. She would like the train to take them in the opposite direction. She desired more than anything else to return to Meiningen into their room and stay there until she knew for sure that there was no danger in her home-coming. Who could do it? The train was taking the young couple farther and farther from the place of their love, dreams, happiness and success.

Lord, have mercy! Lord, have mercy! Lord, have mercy!

To be continued

Autobiography

I was born in 1952 in Ukraine, part of the former Soviet Union. My father was a high ranking military officer in the Soviet army, and my mother was a housewife. My parents tried their best to develop my skills and talents. From five years of age, I remember myself in a tight schedule of different activities, such as musical school, the studio of young actors with acting, dancing and reciting by heart long poems, as well as sport activities. Every Sunday, I had one hour of real leisure, playing chess with my father.

In 1959, I became a student of one of the best schools in our region, where the talented and knowledgeable teachers led us in the world of fascinating knowledge. I can be honest, saying that from ten years of age my teachers and parents motivated me to write. I was an editor of our School Newspaper and in high school – School Newsletter. Most of all I enjoyed to write my personal journal. My daily events were recorded in the form of poems and short stories. On Saturdays, my parents arranged the family candle lit gatherings, where I read my first literary work for them.

During school years, I participated and won multiple essay competitions in Ukrainian and Russian literatures. The language teachers encouraged me to undergo the University studies in journalism and creative writing but I was interested in studying foreign languages. In 1977, I graduated with a diploma and degree, as a specialist of German and English languages and literature.

The years of under and post graduate schools were the most intensive in my life. I was married and became a mother of my son, Roman. My schedule was three times busier, but still there was not a single interesting exhibition, performance, concert, or book that did not reach my attention.

From 1977 to 1988, I worked as a teacher of foreign languages in Ukrainian high school that specialized in studying several foreign languages. I would never forget my classroom of the German and English literatures. The talented artists painted wonderful portraits of world-known authors.

I tried to perform each lesson in a way that my students became the participants of a show and the question of discipline did not exist for me. Who could be bad in it? The world of words, phrases, and grammar phenomena became as interesting as a world of literature, history, and geography of the countries, where people speak English and German. Throughout my professional career, I continued to enjoy writing in journals and exercising my English skills in creative writing. It was not only my favorite leisure interest; it became the preferred hobby of my best students.

In 1988, my family immigrated to the United States where for five years my husband and I fought for the life of our daughter, Tatiana. Eight surgeries with numerous complications and one clinical death proved the words of my mother-in-law: "Ask the Father Almighty when nobody can help, and He will help in His miraculous way." Only God's miracles made our dream come true, and our child survived the hardships of those years.

Our life in the United States dictated new requirements, and I added to my profession the diplomas in holistic medicine and nutrition. God blessed us with over 20 years of successful international wellness practice.

I consider my writing of the family saga *"God's Miracles in Lives of Regular People"* is an alternate historical and inspirational love story about a talented woman with a thorny destiny, and its instant success in the USA and Europe at this difficult time is a real miracle sent from above.

Author Angelic Tarasio

2008

Florida, USA.

Author **Angelic Tarasio**

Photo detail: Painting in the background
of the author is the work of art of His
Highness Duke Michael David Peschka.

Bibliography

Encyclopedias

Encyclopedia Britannica Online, Encyclopedia Britannica, Inc. (2007). Retrieved in 2007, from https:save.britannica.com
> World War II
> Western Ukraine under Soviet and Nazi Rule.

The Columbia Encyclopedia, Six Edition Online Encyclopedia (2007). Retrieved in 2007-2008 from www.highbean.com
> World War II
> Soviet army in Europe
> National Socialism in Germany
> Concentration Camps

Columbia Encyclopedia – Wikipedia, The free encyclopedia. Retrieved in 2007-2008 from en.wikipedia.org/wiki/Columbia_Encyclopedia

Wikipedia: The free encyclopedia, (2007) Wikimedia Foundation, Inc. Retrieved in 2007, from http://www.wikipedia.org
> Ukrainian History: Chronological Table
> Soviet Invasion in Poland

World War II
Ukrainian-German collaboration during WWII
Eastern Front WWII
Kingdom Galicia

Andrew Gregorovich: Retrieved in 2007, from www.infouks.com/history/ww2/
    "Ukrainian History"
    "World War II in Ukraine"

Forum: "A Ukrainian Review"

Leonid Sonnevytsky: BRAMA, Inc. Retrieved in 2007, from www.brama.org/sici?sici=0021
    "Ukrainian History: Chronological Table"
    "History of Ukraine – 20th Century"
    "Annexation of Western Ukraine territory by the USSR"

Harvard University Press Archives: Retrieved in 2007, from www.hup.harvard.edu/catalog/HERJEW.htl

Jeffrey Herf: "The Jewish enemy: Nazi Propaganda during World War II and the Holocaust."

    "Who is Who in World War II." Retrieved in 2007, from www.loc.gov/vets/bib-wwii.html
    New York: Oxford University Press, 1995
    Cambridge: Harvard University Press, 1984

Dictionaries

Webster's Encyclopedic Unabridged Dictionary of the English Language. (1994) 1996 ed. USA, Random House.

Books

The Holy Bible, containing the Old and New Testaments, authorized King James Version, Red Letter Ed. World Bible Publishers.

Prayer Book, Fourth edition, Third Printing with corrections, Holy Trinity Monastery, USA, 2003.

Printed in the United States
By Bookmasters